AF471257

THE HUNTER

MICHAEL CLAYTON

THE HUNTER

Horse, Cob and Pony

COUNTRY LIFE BOOKS

Published by Country Life Books
Holman House, 95 Sheen Road, Richmond upon Thames, Surrey, TW9 1YJ
and distributed for them by
The Hamlyn Publishing Group Limited
London · New York · Sydney · Toronto
Astronaut House, Feltham, Middlesex, England

First published 1980
ISBN 0 600 34592 0

Set in 10 on 12pt Monophoto Plantin by
Tradespools Limited, Frome
Printed in England by
Hazell, Watson & Viney Limited, Aylesbury

CONTENTS

Foreword

BY ULRICA MURRAY SMITH MFH
JOINT MASTER OF THE QUORN

The Country Life Book of the Hunter is a fascinating book, as Michael Clayton is certainly well qualified to write about horse activities. He hunts all over England and Ireland, occasionally in the States too, and no one delights in a good hunt more than he does. He attends all the big shows, and partakes in the new sport of Team Cross Country Events. As Editor of *Horse and Hound* he is untiring in his efforts to help foxhunting and indeed all horse sports.

The Chapter on 'Buying and Caring for your Hunter' is most informative and should help anyone starting a riding career. 'Hunter Breeding', so important today, tells us what the H.I.S. is doing to achieve the right results. I found 'Hunters in the Hunting Field' entrancing, with wonderful descriptions of some of the hunting countries Michael has visited. (A few sound so terrifying that I have no wish to go there!)

An enormous number of people want to go foxhunting, but no season's hunting is going to be much fun without the right sort of mount – this Michael puts very clearly, with many helpful suggestions for the present and the future of the horse world.

It is splendid to have a book which covers so much ground and provides an 'A to Z' on hunters. I am sure that all horse lovers will enjoy this book as much as I have.

Preface

THIS BOOK is an attempt to pay some tribute to all those who have devoted so much of their lives to the cause of producing the hunter, the British riding horse at its best.

It is also one way of saying thank you to the many people throughout the United Kingdom, and in Ireland, who have so generously allowed me to ride their hunters in the course of my tours of hunting countries for 'Foxford's Hunting Diary' in *Horse and Hound*.

All those who have looked after my own hunters so scrupulously also deserve my warmest appreciation.

The hunter makes an enormous contribution to recreational life in the British Isles in so many ways. The type is a priceless national asset, and I hope this book can play at least some small part in encouraging politicians and perhaps business interests to encourage and support the breeding of the riding horse to a far greater extent than is done at present.

I am most grateful to Ulrica Murray Smith, Joint Master of the Quorn since 1959, for writing the Foreword. Mrs Murray Smith's example of high standards and devotion to duty in Mastership would be difficult to surpass.

My special thanks are also due to Gerald Evans, who is such a tower of strength as Secretary of the Hunters' Improvement and National Light Horse Society, for his practical assistance in my researches.

Finally, to all enthusiasts who share an interest in the subject of this book, I offer one sincere wish for the future: good hunting!

Michael Clayton

CHAPTER I

What is a Hunter?

Easier to blow one's horse than one's 'orn.
Mr Jorrocks.

A 'GOOD HUNTER' in my own estimation is simply an animal which carries me successfully across country when I endeavour to follow a pack of hounds. One cannot lay down hard and fast rules about the type of horse that will fulfil this function. Once in the New Forest I dubiously mounted a horse which I immediately dubbed 'the blonde bombshell', a narrow, 15.3 h.h. chestnut gelding from the stable of the late Douglas Coakes. The bombshell duly carried my 6 ft 3 ins and $13\frac{1}{2}$ stone across the Forest with comfort, safety, and the acceleration when required of a motor scooter.

The ideal horse for the country is a 'good hunter'. On the other hand, I was more than a little taken aback in one country when I found myself mounted on a 14.2 h.h. 'show hack'. 'We didn't know you were as tall as that,' my hosts said apologetically. I was the only mounted foot follower out that day. Several times I got my foot kicked out of the stirrup iron by the animal's hind foot, and I had a bizarre feeling that we were going to trip each other up at any moment. Nevertheless, I do recall the so-called 'hack' jumping a swinging iron bedstead with aplomb, for which manoeuvre I tucked my feet up shorter than Lester Piggott.

In many another country I have been fortunate to ride big three-quarter-bred or full Thoroughbred hunters who know their job on the flat or over fences. Indeed, in one country my hosts were so kind that they mounted me on a superb animal which stayed on its feet, gliding like a magic carpet over some of the nastiest, trappiest fences I have ever seen, while around us it looked like a rehearsal for the film version of the Battle of

Waterloo (in which the cavalry did not acquit themselves well, it will be remembered). My immunity owed no credit to any latent skill of mine; I left it all to the horse.

Hunting on horseback outside the United Kingdom and Ireland offers enormous variety in hounds and horses, but the English foxhound and, indeed, the British hunter type horse may be found many thousands of miles from their homeland.

Foxhunting in the United States has a distinguished and parallel history to that of the sport in Britain. The first settlers were frequently foxhunting men, and since the eighteenth century the sport has flourished; in fact it can claim far more varied terrain on the North American continent than anywhere else.

Generalisations are difficult, but it appears that Americans strongly favour full Thoroughbred blood in their hunters, and this is suitable in many of their hunting countries.

Grassland and open rolling terrain are quite often to be found in the American hunting field; the fences where encountered are frequently timber in various forms, and stone walls predominate in some countries.

Neither the hedge and ditch or the Irish bank are mentioned in the official lists of American hunting countries, but some countries do have enormous areas of woodland.

I have so far not had the pleasure of hunting in Virginia and Maryland where so much of the best of American foxhunting has always enjoyed a congenial setting.

Quality horses that can gallop and jump big timber are required here, and the Thoroughbred is often the ideal mount. American horse trials riders and showjumpers use Thoroughbreds at international level, and I have seen this policy pay handsome dividends.

In the 1976 Olympics in Canada, for example, many horses suffered badly from the gradients and dead going on the cross country course in the Three Day Event, performed at Bromont.

American Thoroughbreds had the resilience to cope with the problem, and the use of younger horses than many other teams were riding also paid off for the U.S. team, who carried off both the team and individual gold medals.

Speaking as I find, I would certainly favour full Thorough-

Hunting in snow in the 1978–79 season, the 10th Duke of Beaufort, continuously in office as Master or Joint Master of the family pack since 1924, and amateur huntsman for 47 years. The Duke was born in 1900.

breds to ride after American hounds in many areas. In the South I had some marvellous hunts with the Midland hounds whose huntsman and Joint Master, Mr Ben Hardaway, is one of the most effective hound men I have seen anywhere.

His pack, containing English foxhound and Fell lines as well as some American hound blood, hunts with marvellous voice and drive, and you need a fast horse to stay anywhere near them when they are running on the line of a fox.

Near their kennels at Columbus, Georgia, I followed hounds in dense woodland, and you needed a clever surefooted horse to move fast along the rutted rides out in the forests. Mr Hardaway has another establishment further south in Alabama where the terrain is open, and hounds run like smoke even in temperatures in the nineties. Here, real galloping ability is most necessary in a hunter. We jumped timber rails or chicken coops, filled in wooden triangular obstacles inserted in wire fences, widely used in the American hunting field. I rode a

A magnificent hunter 'chaser, Spartan Missile, ridden by his owner and trainer John Thorne, here being led in after winning the 1979 Horse and Hound Hunter 'Chase Championship at Stratford.

big chestnut Thoroughbred which was an excellent mount.

In Kentucky I hunted with the Iroquois, not on the famous blue grass, but in wooded and hilly country where agility and cleverness were demanded in the horses. There were certainly some Thoroughbreds in the mounted field, but I was exceedingly well mounted on a small horse containing part Appaloosa blood with T.B. cross. He was an excellent ride in this country, a good example of 'horses for courses'.

In New York State I saw a scene much more closely resembling English hunting, except for the distinctive American hounds, when I was fortunate to be invited to join the Millbrook Hunt.

Hounds hunted mainly in woodland, but there is open grass country as well, and the mounted field jumped rails and some stone walls. It reminded me of parts of the Cotswolds. There were far more horses here resembling the English hunter at home, part T.B., and some with considerable substance as well as quality.

Whether hunting the grey American fox, which predominates, the comparatively rarer red English fox, or – as the Arapahoe hunt in Colorado – the coyote, speed and stamina are important in American hunting, and it is not surprising that Thoroughbred blood is so much used in their horses.

Brilliant producer of hunters, Mr David Tatlow, riding the Countess of Inchcape's Figaro to win the Horse and Hound Cup for the hunter championship at the Hunters' Improvement Society Ridden Hunter Show, held on the first day of the Royal Show, Stoneleigh, 1979.

In New Zealand there is no foxhunting, because the fox has never been imported into this sheep rearing country. There are hares, and harrier packs are enthusiastically supported in North and South islands.

New Zealanders are fortunate in that their climate favours the growth of grass throughout the year, except in the far South where the winters are more severe. Hence, horses can be kept out and worked off grass effectively, using the New Zealand rug in the winter months.

The performance and quality of New Zealand bred Thoroughbreds have been accorded increased respect and admiration in recent years. Only the long distance involved in transporting horses to and from the country delayed such recognition. New Zealand racehorses, however, have a fine record on the Australian tracks, winning such a classic as the Melbourne Cup frequently.

I was not surprised, therefore, to see Thoroughbreds among the mounted field out with the harriers. New Zealanders have evolved a simple method of dealing with the barbed wire fences which abound in the vast areas of grass sheep rearing country. Their horses are expected to jump wire, even four or five strands of tightly stretched barbed wire. Aiming at a post was recommended to me when I visited New Zealand, but I noticed that experienced hunters jumped the wire safely well away from the posts.

There is timber and some hedges as well in parts of New Zealand. How fortunate is the horseman in that country; so much grass, and a climate which makes horse keeping so much more economic than in Europe.

There is a little hunting in Australia and Tasmania, and again Thoroughbreds are much favoured.

Drag hunting in South Africa employs Thoroughbreds effectively too, or so I was assured by some sporting gentlemen from the Rand Hunt Club. Distinguished by their white riding caps, which puzzled the Irish natives not a little, I met them out hunting with the Co. Limerick foxhounds.

The Ootacamund Hunt still hunts the jackal in the Nilgiri Hills, Southern India.

On the continent of Europe, the presence of rabies now prevents foxhunting with hounds, but drag hunting abounds in the north European countries, and the French of course hunt deer, hares and wild boar, with hounds.

All these sports tend to be much more 'on the flat' than hunting in England, and hunters of Thoroughbred, or near Thoroughbred, breeding are very much the order of the day.

Comparisons are odious, but in view of the greater expense in buying and keeping horses, how fortunate we are in England and Ireland that so much fun can be obtained in a great many hunting countries on horses of far more plebeian ancestry, with the native ponies and their crosses providing effective mounts for many.

I have had enormous fun in deep, stiffly fenced vales in Dorset, for example, on horses of decidedly common lineage. They would not have kept near hounds in open galloping country, but they jumped big fences boldly and skilfully, and kept coming out sound through gruelling seasons in deep mud.

As long as the hunter can do his job in the country available, no hard and fast rules can be made about his breeding – but the pride of British horse breeding is in fact the Thoroughbred, and his versatility in terrains and climates all over the world is indeed remarkable.

The hunter, as I have indicated, is not a breed, but there is a 'hunter type', best defined in the show ring. The guardian of the hunter type in the United Kingdom is the Hunters' Improvement and National Light Horse Breeding Society, and as I shall explain, the H.I.S. would like to transform the type into a specific breed of British riding horse, but this will take a considerable number of years yet, and demand some drastic extensions to the present system of registering hunters.

Endeavouring to chart the development of the hunter so far has been a considerable task because of its amazing versatility. Apart from carrying riders ranging from small children to veterans in their eighties in the hunting field, the hunter races over fences, show jumps and best of all is an eminently suitable animal for horse trials. There are also a host of other activities which the hunter type performs splendidly, ranging from hunter trials to team cross-country riding, long distance endurance riding and dressage.

We are, in fact, discussing the riding horse at its best. If it has changed in the postwar years the tendency has been towards a general increase in Thoroughbred blood. Point-to-point racing, closely associated with the hunting field, and 'chasing in general have demanded an increased accent on speed rather than solely on jumping ability and a steady gait. The main factor in the change in type, though, has been the decrease in the number of mares of heavier build due to the inevitable decline in the draught horse for farm work and other tasks. As I shall explain in more detail, efforts are currently being made in England and Ireland to remedy this.

The H.I.S. traditionally puts Thoroughbred stallions to a large proportion of non-Thoroughbred mares. Breeding is a dynamic process requiring continual adjustment, but with a constant overall policy. One current school of thought is that the H.I.S. should try using some non-Thoroughbred stallions, perhaps Cleveland Bay or Irish Draught, as a supplement to its list of Thoroughbreds. This, it is argued, should supply the essential element of a good hunter which some feel is increasingly lacking in the modern horse – substance. I am not advocating this, merely reporting it. We have yet to see whether such a plan is possible, and if it produces the desired results.

The H.I.S. is inevitably criticised at times, but no one can deny that it produces particularly good results in horse trials, and has an excellent record in providing successful point-to-pointers and 'chasers when H.I.S. premium stallions are put to Thoroughbred mares. In the 1979 Badminton Three-Day Event, still the toughest annual fixture in the English calendar, four out of the first six horses in the final placings were by H.I.S. stallions: Killaire, the mount of Lucinda Prior-Palmer, who won, is by Carnatic. The others were Jim Wofford's mount Carawich, by Scratchy; Clarissa Strachan's Merry Sovereign, by Galeopsis; and the Queen's Goodwill, ridden by Princess Anne, the handsome brown gelding being by Evening Trial.

In racing areas the H.I.S. can claim such successes as the following horses, by premium stallions: Merryman II, by Carnival Boy, winner of the 1960 Grand National and second in 1961; Specify, by Specific, winner of the 1971 Grand

National – his dam was also sired by a premium stallion; and Highland Wedding, by Question, winner of the 1969 Grand National and three times winner of the Eider Handicap Steeplechase at Newcastle. There are a host of such names, including Charlie Potheen, by Spiritus, winner of the Hennessy Gold Cup and the Whitbread Gold Cup. In the 1975–76 National Hunt racing season, for example, H.I.S.-sired horses scored 136 wins and 223 placings.

The leading show hunter placings are also dominated by premium stallion-sired horses. Every first-prize winner in the Ridden Hunter Classes at the 1976 Horse of the Year Show was in this category.

The horse favoured by the judges in show-hunter classes is that ideal combination of quality and substance which will carry an adult at speed and with safety for long distances over the countryside in the winter months when the going is often deep. It is a mistake, in fact, to think that you automatically need a horse with a modicum of non-Thoroughbred blood to provide the substance. A full Thoroughbred can be a very large horse with plenty of bone, but my word, such types are hard to find nowadays. The priority of the Thoroughbred breeding industry for the racecourse is sheer speed for the flat, and even in the National Hunt sphere there has been considerable concern recently that too many horses are only suitable for hurdling, and that the real 'chaser type is becoming all too hard to find.

What are the judges looking for in the show hunter? Knowing this will give some idea of the 'ideal' which every horseman should have in his mind when he envisages a hunter, which is at best 16 to 16.3 h.h.

As soon as a horse enters a ring it should make its appearance felt by its 'presence', call it star quality if you will, which distinguishes horses just as it does people. The horse with real presence is immediately going to catch the eye of a knowledgeable judge (of course, they are *all* knowledgeable!). Such a horse looks good immediately, seems beautifully proportioned, and has a delightful outlook. It looks bigger as you get close to it.

Now we should consider the horse's parts and limbs separately.

Head and neck Starting at the front end, I believe it is vitally important that a horse has a good eye. Temperament is vital in a working animal, and the eye is one good indication of that factor. A horse with a kind, benevolent eye, which shows signs of intelligence, immediately wins my approval. It makes all the difference between a generous performer and one which is inclined to be 'duck-hearted' or nappy. Small, deeply-placed, piggy eyes are definite drawbacks.

Ideally the head, when viewed from the side, should show a straight profile and not be convex, or Roman nosed, or concave, 'dished'. Although not a beauty, a Roman-nosed horse often has lots of character, even if it will not win in the show ring. Personally I like horses with rather large heads; they seem to be more 'genuine' in personality, but for the show ring the head must not be at all disproportionate. The deformity of the

Hunters at work: part of the Heythrop mounted field during Capt Ronnie Wallace's distinguished Mastership. They are at the start of a good hunt after meeting at Little Compton Manor.

jaw known as 'parrot mouth' is transmitted in breeding and constitutes an official 'unsoundness'.

The angle at which the head is joined to the neck is not only an aesthetic point but is of practical importance. If the angle is too acute the horse is somewhat more inclined to get wind troubles through pressure on the larynx.

The crest of the horse's neck should be arched and long, but it should dip before meeting the withers. When there is no arch of the crest the horse has a 'ewe' neck which inevitably means a bad head carriage. The animal does not bridle well and is less easy to control.

Shoulders The horse's shoulders are vital, and their shape makes a great deal of difference to his performance as a riding horse. Good sloping shoulders are what is desired because you want an easy, free-striding movement. Straight shoulders will limit movement, tending to produce a shorter-striding animal which is not such a comfortable ride and will not have the scope of the longer-striding horse. A conformation fault is the 'loaded shoulder', which means that the shoulder blade, or scapula, has noticeable lumps of muscle.

When you sit on the horse you want to see plenty in front of the saddle; this is what is called a 'good front'. It is reassuring to ride a good-fronted horse if you are jumping sizeable fences, especially those with drops on the landing side.

The withers, just in front of the saddle, should not be wide and flat. They need to be well defined, but a horse with exaggeratedly high withers is a nuisance when it comes to fitting a saddle without causing a sore.

Chest A hunter must have plenty of room for his heart and lungs, otherwise he will never stand a long run across country at a good pace. His chest should be deep, with long ribs, well sprung and spaced well back, so that the edge of the last rib is not too far away from the point of the hip. His forelegs should not look as if they 'come out of the same hole', but they do not want to be too wide apart either, or he will have rather a rolling action which is neither compatible with speed nor comfortable. You want a horse which is 'deep through the heart', with a generous depth from the withers to the elbow.

Forelegs Conformation faults here are particularly serious. Horses so often go lame in front and this is because over half of the animal's weight is carried by the forelimbs, while the back and hind limbs are for propulsion, as explained below.

The horse's elbow should stand well away from the ribs. Tucked-in elbows are obviously a hindrance in free movement of the limb, which is vital. A horse must be free moving to employ a long stride which devours the ground.

The forearm should be long and muscular, so that the knee is 'close to the ground'. Knees should be large and well defined, so that there is plenty of room for leverage. The cannon bone, which goes down below the knee to the fetlock, should be the same width all the way down. When we talk about a horse having 'plenty of bone', we mean the circumference of the cannon bone below the knee, and below the hock at the back. In a hunter there should be at least 200 mm (8 in) of bone; 230 mm (9 in) or more is good. An expert will make a rough and ready guide with his hand as to the amount of bone below the knee.

If the bone just below the knee is narrow, this is called 'tied in', which is a fault. A leg bending slightly back from the knee is called 'calf-kneed' and is not best suited to the action of the knee at full extension, as required when galloping at speed.

The opposite to calf knee is being 'over at the knee', and to a limited extent this is acceptable in a working horse, as horses with this conformation are likely to have less trouble with strained tendons. However, in a show horse, being well 'over at the knee' would certainly be regarded as a fault.

Pasterns should not be of exaggerated slope or length, as this can be a weakness, but if they are too short and upright they increase the effects of percussion.

The fetlocks should be flattish and well defined. The whole foreleg should give an impression of strong, rather flat, flinty bone, and the tendons and ligaments should stand out distinctly. Round, lumpy limbs and joints are much more likely to be heir to unsoundness and show signs of wear.

Back and hind quarters Short-backed horses often have great power and jumping ability but a short-back tends to go with a high action, and can be deuced uncomfortable as you get 'thrown up'. Abnormally long backs, 'slack loins', are worse because they denote weakness. The back needs to be in proportion, therefore, but it should be muscular, broad and deep. A hollow back, or the opposite, an upward-curving back known as a 'roach' back is a conformation fault.

Looking at the bottom line of the body you do not want to see a 'narrow-gutted' beast. The line from the girth back to the sheath should have an upward curve, of course, but it should not curve at too sharp an angle.

The horse's hind quarters should be rounded and give an

impression of power. Viewed from behind, you should see a pear shape, with well developed second thighs below rounded quarters. A 'goose rump' is the name given when a horse's quarters fall away sharply from the top of the pelvis to the dock. A less accentuated form of this is known as a 'jumping bump' and indeed it often does seem to go with the ability to put in an exceptional jump.

The points of the hips, which are the ends of the femurs, or thigh bones, should not protrude sharply, and looked at from behind they should be level. A severely dropped 'pin', as it is sometimes called, can be the result of an accident. This would be badly regarded in the show ring, but from a practical point of view I should add that I have seen horses performing per-

Hunters for the Hodgson family: they come in all sizes but they are all ready to do their job in that great Midlands grass country, the Meynell.

fectly well with this fault in show jumping and in the hunting field.

The muscles of the quarters and the second thigh are vital in helping the horse to propel itself forward and upwards when it is moving on the flat or jumping.

Stifles or patellas At the back end, the stifle should be long, so that it sweeps down to hocks which, like the knees, appear to be close to the ground. A 'slipped' stifle is not uncommon in some immature horses. You should watch to see if the stifle joint works in line with the body and is not thrown outwards each time the horse flexes as it is brought forward.

The point of the hock should form the middle of a straight

line between the point of the buttock and the ground when the horse is standing naturally. In other words, the ideal hind leg is fairly 'straight'.

The hocks must be large and bony. If the inward bend of the hock is excessive it is known as a 'sickle hock' and is likely to suffer from curbs, caused by strain. 'Cow hocks', with which the horse's feet tend to turn outwards, are not desirable because the limbs tend to move out instead of in a straight line. This fault would be badly marked in the show ring, but from a working point of view it is often compatible with a sound performance.

I should add that there can be considerable disagreement as to whether a horse has good or bad hocks; they should be neither too straight nor too sickle, and it is not always easy to assess whether they are just right.

Feet In a hunter feet are of parmount importance. The animal has to perform on all sorts of going, and nowadays will get a lot of percussion. Even in the better hunting countries horses can do too much road work at times, often at a strong canter. I do hate fast work on roads myself, and although it is tempting to follow the other lemmings at this pace, you will often gain very little.

The horse's feet should be neither too large, nor obviously too small. They should be round in front and slightly oval behind. Feet which look 'boxy' are most undesirable and may be an indication of potential navicular disease. The feet must present a level surface, with no rings or grooves which can indicate laminitis. The pad in the centre of the foot, the frog, should be well developed and soft. Shrivelled or shrunken frogs should be treated with considerable suspicion.

Good, healthy, well-shaped feet are not desirable merely for aesthetic reasons, of course. 'No foot, no horse' is one of the oldest and most sensible sayings in the horse world.

CHAPTER 2

Buying and Caring for your Hunter

*Who can expect a perfect 'oss, when he sees what
an infinity of hills they are heir to? Mr Jorrocks.*

IF MONEY is no problem then do not bother to read lengthy
advice on the buying of a horse: just put yourselves in the hands
of a first class dealer. Tell him what you want and the price you
can afford to pay, and he will find you a good hunter. If he is a
sound man he will take it back if you cannot ride it and find you
another one. It is still possible to do this, and I cannot for the
life of me think why some very wealthy people haggle and
dabble when buying horses. They get themselves into a lot of
trouble with bad horses and either end up going to a dealer
anyway, or else they give up the whole idea.

Good dealers can only be found by personal recommendation. There are not as many dealers as there were in the past
because the trade has contracted somewhat at the top end of
the market. Yet it is surprising that some rich folk who would
not dream of buying a cheap, unsafe car, will insist on 'invest-
ing' in risking their necks on horses which they proudly pro-
claim are 'absolute bargains'. The cost, not to say the agony, of
time spent in bed after nasty hunting accidents far outweighs
the extra cost spent on buying a first class hunter from a top
dealer. There are a few rogues among horse dealers, as there
are in all trades, but the man who knowingly sells a bad horse to
a customer is a fool. He is ruining his business, and will not last
long if he wishes to sell horses at top prices.

Sound made horses capable of crossing the Shires and
carrying adults of up to 15 stone take some finding at that. By
the end of the 1970s they were selling at £3,000 plus. If you
wince, just reflect that this is much cheaper than a reasonable

Keen attention from a knowledgeable crowd at the Hunters' Improvement Society's annual show and sale of young stock at Taunton.

family saloon car nowadays, and unlike a car, a good hunter will not only retain his value but even increase it if you look after him, having bought him at say, six to eight years old.

If you cannot afford to take the above course of action, you must realise that 'shopping around' for hunters is a hazardous business, but it can be fun if you have the time and the philosophical temperament for it.

I too get a little impatient with some vendors who advertise in *Horse and Hound* that their precious horses are for sale 'very reasonably', but add sternly that 'time wasters need not apply'. They often have a point, however, as far too many buyers arrive without knowing what they are looking for anyway, and can indeed waste a considerable amount of time by chopping and changing their minds.

Nevertheless, buying from private individuals can be successful if you really know your requirements, and if you have the advice of a knowledgeable person when your own expertise is limited or non-existent. Do not expect a private buyer to take back an unsatisfactory horse, however. Some may, but many will not, and you really cannot blame them. As one old horse dealer used to say to tyro riders: 'I sell the horse, sir, but I cannot sell the rider.' If you cannot get on with the new horse it may be your fault.

Do not rely too heavily on the veterinary profession to carry the can for you. By all means have a veterinary certificate on the horse you intend to buy, and make sure the seller knows you are buying 'subject to vet', but you must realise that nowadays a vet's certificate does not render him liable to be sued if the horse later proves unsatisfactory. He does his best, but the modern tendency to indulge in litigation has persuaded the profession to disclaim legal responsibility for guaranteeing a horse's soundness; they merely offer professional advice.

The other source of hunters is the sales. Those run by the Hunters' Improvement Society have horses ranging from foals to seven-year-olds, but principally they deal with two-, three- and four-year-olds. There is an H.I.S. sale in May at Taunton, another spring sale at Newmarket, and in September there are H.I.S. sales at York and Hereford. These sales are for the produce of the H.I.S. premium stallions under the scheme described later in Chapter 3.

There are also many other hunter sales, all advertised in the pages of *Horse and Hound*. Among the best known are the regular sales at Leicester, with heavy entries of hunters at the beginning and end of the season. Traditionally, Masters of Foxhounds used to sell proven hunters at Leicester at the end of the season, to make a bit of profit and to make way for younger horses. The advantage was that buyers knew something about the hunting country the horses came from, and if they were sound at the end of a season after genuinely carrying a Master or a hunt servant then there was much to be said for their soundness and performance. This still happens, but Masters are finding it difficult to find good young horses and are tending to keep their hunt horses longer nowadays, although retiring Masters still regularly send good horses to Leicester.

Another way of obtaining good horses has been to buy Thoroughbreds at the sales where 'chasers are sold; Ascot or Doncaster are favourite places for this. You really need to know exactly what you are doing to succeed at this game, but some splendid bargains may be achieved, provided you do not need a horse up to too much weight. A 'chaser soured of racing may go quite reasonably at a sale, but you are taking a gamble on his hunting potential.

If I hunted on one of the moorland countries, such as Exmoor, I think I might try buying Thoroughbreds in this way. There is no jumping on Exmoor, so it does not matter if the ex-racehorse is not much of a fencer, but galloping is important on the moor and some blood horses will take to it very well indeed, and their speed will enable you to stay with the hounds. But it *is* a gamble.

Once you are looking for a hunter type with form as an eventer, show jumper, or point-to-pointer then the price can easily soar and this is not surprising.

Your best bet for the 'reasonable' buy is to acquire a young horse and 'make' him yourself, provided you have the time and the knowledge to achieve this. With the right advice, it is worth trying, but there are disappointments as well as a great deal of fun in bringing on young horses.

Ireland is traditionally a great source for the hunter type. Prices have sky-rocketed there because of the competition from continental and other buyers seeking top class show jumpers and eventers. However, some British dealers still bring over batches of Irish-bred horses and sell them on here. Remember that an Irish horse usually takes at least six months to a year to acclimatise properly to English conditions, but a good one will be a friend indeed in the hunting field if you give him time to settle down.

A growing trend in Ireland and in England is for sales of hunter-type horses to be accompanied by demonstrations of the horses' ability over show jumps. This is being done in Dublin, at Stoneleigh in Warwickshire, and elsewhere. If you are stuck for sources to buy hunters in England and Ireland contact either the Hunters' Improvement Society or the Irish Horse Board (see page 172).

The great boon of the old-fashioned dealer was that he would allow customers of repute and means to try horses in the hunting field. This is splendid if you can persuade a vendor to allow it, but I doubt whether it is a facility easily obtained nowadays. Nevertheless, do make every effort to give your prospective purchase a proper riding trial yourself if you are buying it privately or from a dealer. I once made rather a bad mistake in not really galloping a horse properly. He was perfectly sound, but when I got him among other horses in the hunting field I realised that he was desperately slow. He had not been sold as a fast horse, but I had not expected him to be quite so sluggish, and no matter how fit he became he never had the 'foot' for the job and I sold him on as a confidential type.

In Chapter 1 I have endeavoured to describe the ideal shape of the hunter type. You will also want to examine your prospective purchase for any peculiar lumps and bumps. Do get an expert to help you, but it is worth knowing why he is running his hands over the horse's legs.

A splint is one of the most common problems which occur in horses; it is a deposit of bone which forms on the splint bone and which can be seen and felt as a hard lump. It causes unsoundness when it is forming, but usually settles down after that, although some horses do suffer sporadic trouble with splints thereafter. Large unsightly ones can all too easily be knocked and even fractured, causing much more lameness.

Below the fetlock, on the pastern, a hard ridge may be an indication of ringbone, one of the most serious causes of chronic lameness. The symptoms of such a condition can all too easily be masked nowadays by giving the drug phenylbutazone to a horse, and the pain will not recur until the effects of the drug have worn off some days later, by which time, if you are buying the horse, it may be too late.

The same is true of the chronic conditions inside the foot, such as navicular disease or pedal ostitis. There are external manifestations when the disease is advanced, such as a contracted outer hoof and an abnormally concave sole. In the early stages, however, there are virtually no external signs. For these reasons it is becoming increasingly common for purchasers buying expensive horses to ask their veterinary surgeon to X-ray the feet when he examines the horse before the sale.

Most of these foot ailments are associated with a lot of percussion on the forefeet due to a great deal of road work. Driving horses are especially likely to suffer from them for this reason.

When examining the hind legs it is well to remember that the hocks are subject to numerous problems, and a hunter's hocks are vitally important. It is here that much of the strain of jumping is felt.

A curb is a blemish sometimes found even on a well-shaped hock. It takes the form of a hard swelling on the back of the hock, about 75 mm (3 in) below the point of the hock. Curbs when fired do not often give trouble again.

On the lower inside of the hock you may find a bone spavin. This is a bony deposit not always easy to detect. Compare the two hocks by feeling them. If they differ in size, then you have a clue as to this form of unsoundness. It may not be causing lameness at the time, but it is a sign of a strain, and the cure is either a lot of rest or firing. Either way you do not want to buy a horse with this problem.

Bog spavin is a soft swelling which also occurs on the inside of the hock, but in a higher position. Unless the swelling is large it is not necessarily a very serious matter, but technically it does constitute an unsoundness.

Looking at the feet again, take the trouble to be sure that they are in proportion to the size of the horse, neither large like a soup plate, nor small and narrow like those of a donkey. They should be round and hard – and form a pair at the front and back.

Trying a horse requires concentration. When you first mount him, do not bump away into a trot immediately. Sit there and have a quiet walk. You will find out much better this way if the horse is sensitive to the pressure of the leg, how he feels on the hand, and something about his temperament. Make his acquaintance and get on terms with him. Then you can give him a trot, and a little later let him have a canter. Gradually and imperceptibly allow him to slip into a balanced gallop. As I have intimated, it is most important to see whether a hunter can gallop. As one expert put it: 'If you feel a lot of movement under you, and you see his knees instead of his toes, you will know he cannot be very fast.' Ease him up from the gallop quietly and gently. You should ask if you can give him a jump, but do not expect too much from a hunter in cold blood. It is not the same as buying a trained show jumper. Nevertheless, you will want your horse to jump reasonably boldly and to give you a 'good feel'. You need not jump an enormous obstacle to test his prowess; about 1 metre (3 ft 4 in) will be sufficient. If possible try to put him over one or two varied obstacles if they are available and not just the one which the owner immediately provides for you.

The spring is a good time to buy a 'made' hunter. He should have completed a season sound, and will not have had a summer to recover from injuries received the previous season, as would be the case if you bought him in the autumn. You have the summer to get to know him; hack him about quietly, if you can, and then you can get him fit in the autumn for the season ahead.

This is not a complete horsemastership manual, but the care of hunters for the hunting field has one or two special points which are worth noting.

The hunter's regime has remained basically unchanged over the last 250 years: he lives indoors in winter and works in the

Buyers from Holland study a hunter to be sold at Leicester's famous end of season sales. Leading this horse is Mrs Dermot Kelly, wife of the former Master and huntsman of the Meynell and South Staffs Hunt.

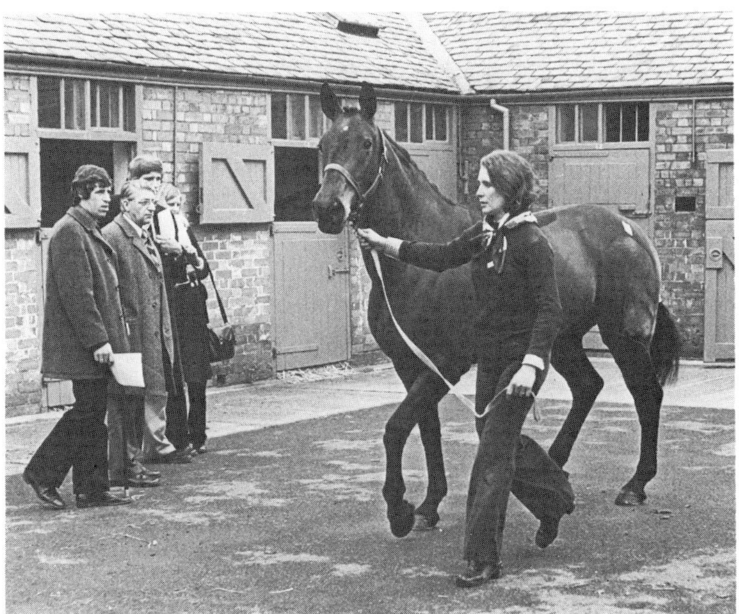

hunting field; in the spring he is turned out to grass 'for a rest' and he comes in again in the autumn to resume work.

Whilst it is true that some sort of a rest after a hard season is a good idea, and green grass is a tonic, it has long been debated as to whether we really need to let the hunter down in condition so completely during the summer months. The reason we do it is basically a hard economic one: it is cheaper that way. The alternative would be to keep him in at night, but out by day to get some grass, and never let him get completely unfit. There is quite an acceptable argument that the system otherwise puts a great strain on a horse's digestive system by making a major change twice a year from hay, corn, bran etc., solely to grass, and then back again. It could also be argued that too many people are inclined to put the poor beast out to grass at the end of the hunting season night and day, no matter what the weather is doing. Cold, wet springs are not uncommon in the British Isles and really big horses which have been clipped all winter seldom have a natural coat when they are turned out, even if they have been roughed off for several weeks. Wind troubles the following season could all too easily be attributable to being turned out too early the previous spring in cold weather.

It is wise, therefore, to interpret the basic system as generously as possible in favour of the horse. When you bring him up from grass give him *plenty* of time to get fit again; when you turn him out in the spring wait until the weather is milder. These are not sentimental precautions, but good investments in your hunter having a long working life.

I like my horses to come up from grass at the beginning of August. The best of the grass is finished by then, and the flies and stamping about on hard going which may occur at that time of year do not benefit a hunter. If the weather turns really hot in August it is worth bringing a horse in by day and turning it out at night, even if you are not going to work it.

The horse needs to be wormed soon after he resumes full stable routine. Allow him a little grass in his box for some days while you transfer him to a diet of hay and a hard feed of perhaps 1.3 kilos (3 lbs) of oats a day. Start getting him fit with light walking exercise and then gradually build up the walking regime to as much as two hours a day. It should be at least three weeks before you start trotting. Even when you do start trotting the horse, I do not believe in a great deal of banging about on the roads at a hard trot, for the sake of tendons and feet. Keep him walking on the roads, and trot a bit when you get to softer going.

Whilst out at grass you should have kept a careful check on his feet. In a dry summer when the ground gets hard a horse's feet may easily split, and ideally they should get some attention from a farrier during the summer. This seldom happens nowadays, but the feet must certainly be given attention once the horse comes in.

As the horse becomes more fit he will need more hard food. During this period he will require more than 6.3 kilos (14 lbs) of hay a day, and you should build up to whatever level of oats you feel is judicious. Some people stuff up to 7 kilos (16 lbs) of oats a day, or even more, into a really fit hunter when he is in full work. No two horses are the same, of course, and many will 'do' better on much less than this. Furthermore, oats go to a horse's head like champagne, some being affected by them more than others. There is no point in corning up a horse to the limit if it makes him behave like a fool all day.

I am sure horses last longer if they do two half days a week rather than one long, severe day. For two half days a week a horse would not need corning up so much, and he is much less likely to return to the stable over-tired, or exhausted.

It will take at least six weeks to get him anywhere near properly working fit, and you should remember this if you are taking him cubhunting after he has been in from grass for only three weeks or so. Go as a mounted spectator and walk about, but do not do any fast work at this stage, and do not keep the horse out for a long cubhunting morning. It is preferable not to take him cubhunting until he really is much fitter.

All my remarks are directed to the conditioning of the big Thoroughbred, or near Thoroughbred, hunter. Ponies and small cobs will usually get fitter much more quickly, but you can also damage them by hurrying things too much.

Once you get your hunter up to his full oat ration he will need less than 6.3 kilos (14 lbs) of hay a day; probably nearer

4.5 kilos (10 lbs). Most stables feed three times a day: four smaller feeds is a better programme if you can manage it. Horses are grazing animals, and even indoors they benefit from a 'little and often' policy.

Here is a suggested four-times-a-day menu for a large hunter, over 16 h.h., when in full work:

At each feed give 900–1800 grams (2–4 lbs) of oats, mixed with chaff; bran can be mixed with the oats in at least two feeds; supply 900–1800 grams (2–4 lbs) of hay with each feed.

Once a day give 900 grams (2 lbs) of horse nuts in addition.

Twice a week substitute a boiled feed for one of the corn feeds. This can include: 225 grams ($\frac{1}{2}$ lb) boiled linseed; 900 grams (2 lbs) boiled barley; 450 grams (1 lb) steamed oats; 225 grams ($\frac{1}{2}$ lb) steamed bran. Give a bran mash once or twice a week, but not the night before hunting. Make a bran mash with 1350 grams (3 lbs) bran, 28 grams (1 oz) salt and 1.5 litres ($2\frac{1}{2}$ pints) of boiling water. Leave it for 20 minutes to cool before feeding.

Horses, like humans, get bored with monotony, some more

Brood mares in the sunshine: one of the classes in the Hunters' Improvement Society's annual summer show at Shrewsbury for brood mares and young stock, shown in hand.

than others. It is a good thing to brighten up the menu with occasional grated carrots or swedes. Cod liver oil may also be added to feeds, especially after Christmas.

When a horse comes in from hunting give him a gruel of oatmeal or pearl barley – 450 grams (1 lb) of meal to 4.5 litres (a gallon) of water, stir and allow to simmer. Alternatively give linseed tea – 225 grams ($\frac{1}{2}$ lb) of linseed boiled in 4.5 litres (1 gallon) of water. The horse can have his normal feed later in the evening. *All* linseed fed to horses must be boiled before feeding: otherwise it can be toxic.

You can buy a whole range of additive vitamin preparations if your horse is a shy or difficult feeder and does not 'do' well. Some hunters undoubtedly worry the flesh off, pacing about in the box after hunting and mentally jumping the fences again.

Nowadays oats and bran are expensive, and the latter is often difficult to obtain. Fiddling about making up feeds is time consuming. If you are doing the horse yourself, and have a lot of other things to do, it is worth trying complete horse cubes instead. If you employ labour which is not particularly skilled it is probably even more worthwhile to use horse cubes. I was very dubious about it when one of my horses was put on to this system for the first time, but he flourished on them, and behaved far more sensibly than on an oats diet. The makers give detailed instructions as to the amounts and types of horse nuts applicable to your horse, depending on his size and the work he is doing. The nuts contain a fibre content and all essential vitamins and minerals in a complete balanced ration. I do not think it is cheaper than the traditional methods in cash, but it does save time, and requires much less expertise.

The best time to give your hunter his first clip of the season is probably the first week in October. I believe in clipping right out on the first occasion, leaving the legs and saddle patch only on the second and subsequent clippings. Give your horse an extra blanket after his first clipping.

When I hunted in Dorset and the Cotswolds there always seemed to be plenty of water about to give a horse's legs a good splashing at the end of the day's hunting. If this is so it is essential to give him a trot up afterwards to dry off.

Standing in his stable with wet or muddy legs is the way a horse contracts mud fever. By all means wash his legs and feet at home with a hose, but they *must* be dried off afterwards. The trouble is that with shortage of labour, or ill-trained labour, in too many modern stables, horses are left standing after hunting far too long with wet or muddy legs. As soon as they have been dried off his legs should be carefully inspected for thorns or wounds.

Make sure his water has the chill off it (add boiling water to a bucket of cold) when he gets in. Let him crop at his hay net while you get the worst of the mud off his belly, then wipe his eyes, nose and sheath, and take special care to clean the mud from inside his hind legs. Bandage his legs after cleaning and drying them, ideally using a lining of cotton wool or tissue to absorb any moisture. Dry his loins and his ears with care.

Now the horse should be reasonably comfortable and you can give him his warm feed, leaving him in peace to eat it. Check later to see if he has broken out into another sweat; if so dry him off again, using a straw wisp and a rubber. Many horses get cold ears at such a time, and I have many a time rubbed them warm again while my hunter stands with his head down, much appreciating the attention.

Next morning you will complete the full grooming, and have another good look for signs of sprains or swellings. Take him out of his box and walk, then trot, him up the yard to see if he is going sound. Then put him back in his box and give him the day off. Normal exercise can be resumed the day after.

Once a horse is hunting fit he does not need much more than fifty minutes slow exercising out of the stable on the days between hunting, but give a pleasant strong canter the day before he hunts to clear his wind.

In the sale ring at Leicester, a hunter from the Woodland Pytchley country under close scrutiny before coming under the auctioneer's hammer. The hunter trade is a basic element in Britain's busy equine market.

Considering all the time and trouble taken in keeping and feeding a hunter, it is amazing that some people do not devote that extra bit of attention to ensuring that their horses are well turned out at the meet. It is a compliment to the Master and to the farmers and landowners on whose land you will hunt if your horse – and you – are smartly turned out, with your mount clipped, plaited up, and with hooves shining with hoof polish.

There are several precautions I think are essential for horse-owners nowadays. You will probably have your horse inoculated against tetanus; *do* make sure that he is also given anti-flu injections. The latter is increasingly important because the greater mobility of horses nowadays means that equine flu is sweeping Britain in the winter months far more widely. If your horse starts that dreadful cough, or goes off his feed with a high temperature, he has probably got flu. It will mean at least five or six weeks off work, and there is a risk of damaging him with fast work even after that. At a crucial time of the year this can rob you of the best part of the hunting season.

I *do* recommend insuring hunters, especially if you have only one or two: the premiums give all sorts of variations in the use to which you put your horse. Hunters are expensive to replace suddenly, and the expression 'as strong as a horse' is one of the most misleading in the English language. Your 'strong' horse is vulnerable to so many ills and accidents, and some policies will even allow you to insure against some of the veterinary bills.

If you really do not have all the proper facilities, nor the time, to do a hunter well during the season, it is silly to try. Far better to put him in a really good hunter livery yard. The best ones are not cheap; but if you add up the costs of employing labour, maintaining stables, and many other factors, keeping a horse at livery is not a bad bargain.

Rely on strong personal recommendation in finding a good livery stable. The golden rule, whether your hunter is at home or at livery, is to treat him like a living being, a friend not a machine. It is not difficult to spot whether he is in good condition or bad, whether he is happy or unhappy. Always look at him with these questions in mind – and if all is not well, do something about it straight away.

CHAPTER 3

Hunter Breeding

If his 'oss is not so good as it might be, let him
cherish the reflection that it might have been far
worse! *Mr Jorrocks.*

As we have already seen, the best hunter is often a cross-bred
animal, with a high proportion of Thoroughbred blood.
Breeding Thoroughbreds for the racecourse, in theory, at
least, gives the breeder the inestimable advantage of the General
Stud Book, maintained since 1791. Enormous research can be
done when matings involving many thousands of pounds in
stud fees are arranged in the hope of producing the blue-
blooded winners of classic races.

The simplest way of summing up the problems of the breeder
using non-Thoroughbred blood is the response of the Irish
dealer to the buyer who enquired as to the parentage of the
horse he had just bought. 'Who would you like him to be by?'
rejoined the Irishman with a conspiratorial grin.

Hunter breeding has long been a pragmatic process, but it
was partially successful in a haphazard way in the eighteenth
and nineteenth centuries, and indeed well into this century,
because breeders had virtually only one market for the hunter –
the hunting field itself, although the better end of that market
would be expected to cater for point-to-pointing and hunter
'chasing as well. The cavalry was an associated market, but it
needed exactly the same type as the hunting field. It is worth
noting that the immense demand for driving horses before the
advent of the motor vehicle was also associated with the hunter
market. Many a driving horse did duty in the hunting field as
well, and performed extremely successfully. Otho Paget, *The
Field*'s great hunting correspondent, recalled that in 1880 he
commenced hunting regularly with the Quorn on a 15h.h.

41

mare which he bought cheaply from the local butcher. Remember that the Quorn country was then a paradise of old turf, but Paget reported that his mare galloped and jumped brilliantly.

In this century the competitive role of the hunter type has broadened enormously, with the good class riding horse being so much in demand for show jumping, horse trials and dressage. The difference in hunter breeding since the Second World War has become more marked as the demands for competition horses have grown, commanding prices well above the levels expected for horses bought for the hunting field. Indeed, we have now arrived at a situation where all too frequently it is said of a young horse's prospects: 'Oh well, if he can't do anything else, he'll just have to make do as a hunter.' This is an attitude which is depressing, even tragic, to those who see the hunting field as the scene of the horse's greatest glory, the place where he can prove himself to the full. Yet the remark is born out of economics and expediency, the millstones on which many an ideal is crushed.

As explained in Chapter 1, Thoroughbreds often perform brilliantly in the hunting field, but economics dictate that a great many Thoroughbreds cannot be bred primarily for hunting. They find their way into this sphere because they have proved unsuitable for racing, or have become soured or too old for the racecourse. The evolution of the English Thoroughbred owed everything to the importation of Arab blood. Thoroughbreds of contemporary breeding can be traced in male line through about thirty generations to the three famous sires, the Byerley Turk, the Darley Arabian and the Godolphin Arabian.

Then the crossing of Thoroughbred stallions with draught horses produced the horse with quality and substance which is the essence of the hunter. The Cleveland Bay, Shire, Clydesdale and Suffolk Punch have all been used as hunter dams; in Ireland the Irish Draught horse is a superb foundation stock, and we will explore the breeding of the Irish hunter later.

In the nineteenth century the British cavalry favoured the Thoroughbred hunter for its stamina and speed. The improvement in Thoroughbred breeding due to the Arab importations had enabled this type of cavalry horse to evolve from the very heavy animal used in Cromwell's Model Army.

Up to the mid-eighteenth century staghunting was the premier form of venery, but the clearance of many of the great forests to meet more modern farming requirements encouraged hunting men to favour the fox as a quarry. Foxhounds could provide shorter but faster runs in the open. Leicestershire proved to be the most suitable county for foxhunting; its light, upland soil drains easily, and the great grazing grounds of Leicestershire and the area which used to be Rutland provide good scenting countries.

In the early nineteenth century the hunter was required to perform a far different task to the role which it had filled for most of the previous hundred years. Enclosure of land in the late eighteenth century had produced timber or hedges as boundaries which had to be crossed by horses if their riders were to stay near hounds. The pace of hunting quickened enormously. A Mr Childe, known as Flying Childe, introduced the practice of taking fly fences at a gallop when following the hounds of Mr Meynell, who was Master of the Quorn and the founder of modern foxhunting practice. Previously hunters had been required only to leap ditches and occasional vertical

Bred in Ireland: at Clonmel Horse Show, a good example of a half bred brood mare and her prize-winning filly foal by Regal Record. The mare is Mr John Carrigan's Tawny Bay.

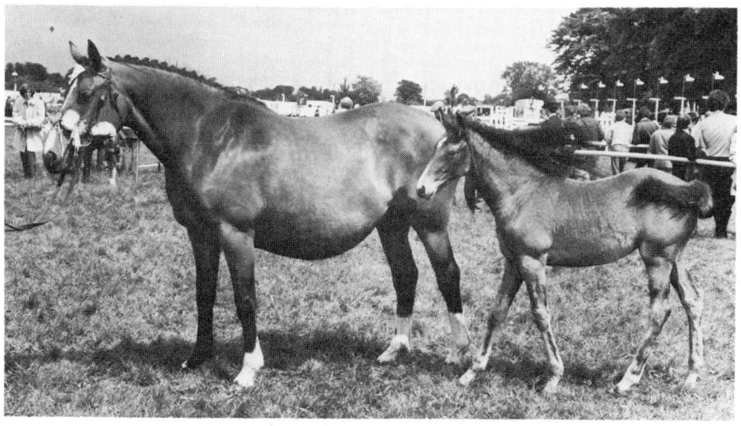

obstacles, the technique being usually to 'crane' first, and then jump virtually from a standstill. The introduction of hedges and ditches precluded this method, and so more Thoroughbred blood was used in hunter breeding as the pace of the sport increased. Incidentally, the rise of foxhunting coincided with the increase in the manoeuvring pace in the cavalry.

I referred earlier to the 'partial success' of haphazard breeding methods because towards the end of the nineteenth century it had become all too clear that there was a serious dearth of quality riding horses. It has been estimated that such was the shortage of these horses that in the ten years up to 1882 nearly £7 million was spent abroad in importing horses into Britain. Translated into modern currency values this was an immense sum, and there was considerable concern about the problem. To try to alleviate it, in 1885 the Hunters' Improvement and National Light Horse Breeding Society was formed. Its aim was to 'improve and promote the breeding of hunters and other horses used for riding or driving, and for general purposes'.

The formation of the H.I.S. was one of the best things that ever happened to equestrianism in Britain. Everyone who enjoys the riding horse owes the Society an immense debt. It has been the guardian of the hunter type, surviving all the vicissitudes inevitable during and after two world wars, and all the immense social and econimic changes which have so affected the horse world. Today the H.I.S. is more important than ever, even though, as I shall explain, it is hampered by a serious lack of financial support compared with the horse-breeding industries of Ireland, France and West Germany.

When the H.I.S. first started its role of making available to breeders good sound Thoroughbred stallions at moderate fees, it evolved the premium scheme which is still run today in a more expanded form. In 1888 eight premiums, or subsidies, each of £50, were awarded to suitable stallions and the covering fee was £2. Each of the eight premium stallions covered twenty mares. By 1923 twenty-eight premiums of £150 were offered and today the figure has risen to sixty-two premiums valued at a minimum of £650, rising to over £1,000 for the best horse in the annual stallion show.

Before a stallion is accepted for entry at the show it must be

With the famous yellow caravan which toured so many horse shows and other events to fly the banner on behalf of hunter breeding is the late Major-General Sir Evelyn Fanshawe, and his assistant Mrs Betty Townsend.

first be licensed by the Ministry of Agriculture and must be free of the following: cataract, roaring, whistling, ringbone, sidebone, bone spavin, navicular, shivering, stringhalt, and defective genital organs. A certificate must be produced stating that the animal has not been tubed or hobdayed, and is not parrot-mouthed. Since the disastrous outbreak of contagious equine metritis, which hit the Thoroughbred breeding industry so hard in 1977, the H.I.S. has required all stallions to be swab-tested for this disease, the regulation also applying to the mares they cover. Much trouble is taken to ensure that the Society is breeding from sound, healthy stock.

Despite the early efforts of the H.I.S. the subject of horse breeding continued to cause sporadic alarm in Westminster because of the cavalry's needs. In 1908 there was a Royal Commission on Horse Breeding and in a subsequent debate in the House of Lords on its findings there were grave warnings about shortages of cavalry mounts. It was estimated there were then 2,087,000 horses in the United Kingdom, of which 150,000 were fit for cavalry use. This is an interesting figure,

The Hunters' Improvement Society stallion show, held annually in March at Newmarket. At this show the vital premiums are awarded to stallions selected by distinguished judges.

since these horses would largely be working hunters, or potential hunters. The Government talked hopefully about registering 'suitable stallions and mares' to produce the right types of horse for the cavalry, but of course the horrors of the First World War were just around the corner. The horse certainly played a large part in the First World War as a draught animal, but mechanisation of the Army was under way.

The task of endeavouring to raise the standards of non-Thoroughbred breeding remained largely in the hands of the H.I.S. Its council was mainly composed of gentlemen with hunting and military backgrounds, who performed impeccably the role originally envisaged. The background of the Society's leading lights, and its aims, have remained remarkably constant. Tradition and unity of purpose are excellent ingredients in a breeding policy, and the H.I.S. is fortunate in retaining these assets. It should not be imagined however, that its path is one of

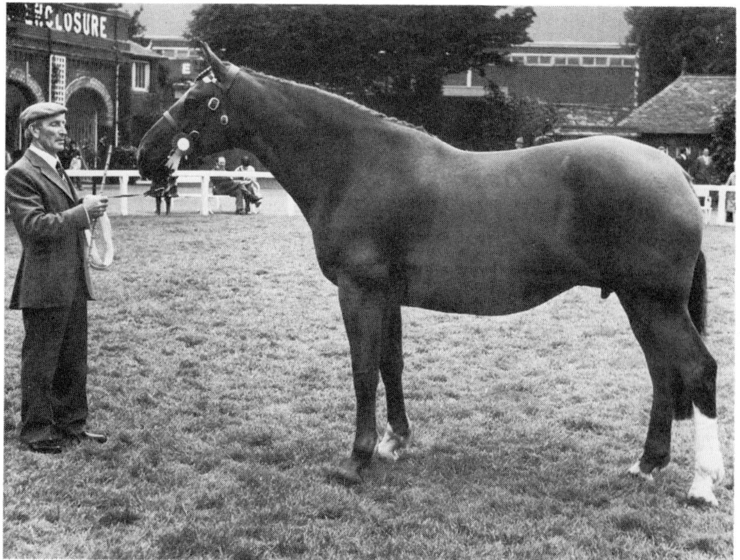

One of the great foundation stock sources for the hunter – a splendid example of an Irish Draught mare. Mr Joseph Farrell is showing Baltic, a champion at the Dublin Horse Show.

unbroken tranquillity. Breeding is a dynamic process and there are bound to be differences of opinion about current and future policy. The Society's role as the arbiter of hunter showing also ensures that heat and light are generated occasionally in the sort of row which is part and parcel of the show ring.

A splendid row raged when the H.I.S. ruled in 1974 that animals which had been hobdayed or otherwise operated on for their wind would no longer be eligible for entry in any hunter classes. There was much controversy over one leading horse at the time.

There were howls of protest. The objectors said it was absurd to ban such horses. They claimed that large hunters were inevitably subject to wind trouble. The hobday operation was not an unsoundness, but a cure for an unsoundness.

There is no cure for a horse which is broken-winded due to lung damage or emphysema, but a blockage of the air passage in the throat may be relieved by the Hobday surgical operation. A blockage occurs in the following way. The nerves which serve the horse's larynx or voice box become paralysed, especially on the left side. This means that a flap attached to the larynx becomes inactive. Normally it moves backwards and forwards as the horse breathes. However, when paralysed the flap lies partly or completely across the larynx and interferes with the passage of air being drawn down into the lungs. This produces sounds varying from whistling to a sort of roar when the horse breathes in. Relief of this nerve paralysis by surgery can partially or completely return the horse's breathing to normal, and enable it to return to strong work such as hunting or racing. A side effect is that the horse loses the power to whinny. Afterwards it can be extremely difficult to spot that a hobday operation has been performed. There is only a small scar on the underside of the neck, and it can hardly be detected by feeling for it. Tubing a horse as an alternative is all too easy to spot. It

A great personality of the hunter world, and a great horse: Mr Charlie Mumford with his stallion Quality Fair, having just won the King George V Challenge Cup at the Hunters' Improvement Society stallion show for the fourth time.

involves surgically inserting a special tracheotomy tube into the horse's windpipe. This is unsightly and the horse makes a noise, but undoubtedly it works well in many cases.

The H.I.S. Council stuck to their guns on the Hobday issue, and the ban has continued. I think they were justified because there does seem to be a hereditary predisposition towards the laryngeal paralysis among horses with exceptionally 'big fronts'. A good front, in the form of big sloping shoulders and a large neck, is practical in that it is part of the conformation of a large, free-moving horse. If carried to excess, however, the animal with a big, swan-like neck does appear to be far more susceptible to wind troubles. Such animals look well in the show ring, but this is the classic trap into which one can fall when endeavouring to breed too closely to type. In dog shows we see animals with exaggerated breed characteristics which require all sorts of veterinary attention to overcome such problems as slipped discs, or breathing problems in flat-nosed animals such as pekes or boxers. The horse is, thank heaven, still primarily a working animal and aesthetic considerations must always give way to practical needs.

Another row broke out in 1975 when a champion hunter, and indeed the champion horse, of the Royal International Horse Show had its awards subsequently removed when a dope test revealed that the animal showed traces of phenylbutazone, the pain-relieving drug. The H.I.S. firmly forbids the administration of any form of drug to show hunters. As a breed society its task is to encourage the production of sound animals, and the surest way to defeat this object is to breed from horses which have defects masked by the use of drugs.

The subject remains a controversial one in the horse world and has considerable relevance to the hunter type. The Jockey Club forbids the use of phenylbutazone, or 'bute' as it is known, in all horses running under Rules on the flat or over fences in the United Kingdom. The relationship between performance on the racecourse and decisions made about future matings is crucial to the science of Thoroughbred breeding. In America bute is allowed in some states but not in others, and there are considerable problems over the 'medication' of American race-horses which are not assisted by serious anomalies of this sort.

At the time of writing the International Equestrian Federation, the F.E.I., continues to allow bute to be used in show jumpers and horses taking part in horse trials. This has caused storms of contention, particularly in relation to three-day events. The critics say that it makes a nonsense of a trial if the horses competing are sound only with the aid of drugs. They point out that the tendency for owners to use bute as an insurance against a sound horse going lame is even more reprehensible. It means that if the horse strikes itself or is otherwise injured during the speed and endurance phase then the immediate effects may be masked. Thus 'protected' the horse appears to be sound at a veterinary inspection before the final phase of a three-day event, the show jumping.

Bute is usually administered in the form of powders, given in the feed daily to build up and maintain its pain-killing properties. The drug does seem to have a therapeutic effect on some muscular strains, but it is not basically a curative medicine. Slight damage to tendons would normally cause immediate signs of lameness in a horse during a three-day event, but thoroughly armed with bute, the animal may not show any signs of trouble until the administration of the drug has been discontinued for several days. What might have been a comparatively light injury, cured by instant rest, is much aggravated and the working life of the horse may all too easily be shortened.

It is now estimated that an event horse is unlikely to have a working life at top international horse trials level of more than four or five seasons, such are the strains and stresses of this demanding sport. The opponents of bute complain that the use of the drug is making this problem more acute, and it is not assisting the breeding of sound stock, since mares which have competed with the aid of drugs may well be used for breeding when their competitive life is over, and may all too easily transmit their weaknesses to future young stock.

It must be conceded, though, that bute is sometimes most effective in arthritic bone conditions. Navicular disease and pedal ostitis are foot conditions which can be sufficiently alleviated by bute to allow a horse several more seasons' work. The defenders of the drug say that it would be foolish to ban something which prolongs active life in this way, since the alternative would be to put down a chronically lame horse.

In my view, there is no justification for allowing bute to remain an exception among the drugs which are banned in competitive contests. There are other drugs of even greater sophistication constantly being developed. All drugs should be banned for three-day eventing; I am less sure about show jumping, since an exceptional show jumper does not reach his peak until he is well into maturity, or even old age in some cases. By this time he may well have developed a foot problem. He is not called upon to perform at the same levels of stamina and speed as an eventer.

The other solution to lameness problems is neurectomy, or de-nerving the foot, which involves the severing of certain sensory nerves. It is a drastic measure, but it certainly works exceedingly well in some cases. Extremely successful show jumpers have continued to perform brilliantly for a surprising number of seasons after de-nerving operations.

Mr Charlie Mumford and his triple champion of the H.I.S. Stallion Show, Bleep, a son of Pinza from a Hyperion mare.

Mrs H. S. Jeff's My Rougette, by Longton Heath, champion brood mare at the Hunters' Improvement Society's National Hunter Show at Shrewsbury, 1979.

The F.E.I. decided at its annual assembly in December, 1978, to reconsider the problem two years later in the light of further veterinary research into the side effects of bute. There have been allegations that the drug can cause a horse's bones to become unnaturally brittle, but so far there has not been conclusive evidence of this. Those countries, including Germany, which opposed bute were less inclined to press the matter when it became clear that the Federation would not ban bute without at the same time forbidding de-nerving. This operation is said to be widely used in Germany and elsewhere on the continent.

I have discussed the drugs problem at some length since it is a vital matter associated with modern horse breeding. It will become more acute as the drugs industry produces ever more extraordinary, not to say frightening, short-term miracles. Their long-term effects on the future development of a breed could be catastophic. The horse has arrived at its present partnership with man after centuries of use as a working animal. If it has failed to match up to its role it has not been used as breeding stock. Stallions obviously need to be of good conformation and impeccable soundness, yet it is too often overlooked that mares also transmit hereditary dispositions to unsound conditions as well as conformation faults.

As we shall see in more detail, the greatest problem in hunter breeding in Britain, and until recently in Ireland has been the lack of effective registration of mares. This means that it is virtually impossible to record and impose levels of soundness and conformation on mares put to Thoroughbred stallions to achieve the hunter type. I have so far only mentioned the pain-killing drugs, but other medications used to 'assist' horses could have even more dramatic effects in upsetting nature's methods of selectivity in producing sound stock. This applies in particular to the use of steroids in young stock to evoke abnormal growth and muscle development, which can only be condemned.

Tranquillisers and stimulants are of course banned in all competitive horse sports. The former is the more likely to be used, and a new drug has recently emerged from America which apparently has extraordinary properties in quietening horses. A leading American show jumper was temporarily suspended and fined for using this drug. It is a method of cheating in an equestrian competition to attempt to achieve by drugs what should be attained by horsemanship. If the animal is unable to compete successfully without the aid of a tranquilliser then it is not fit to take part, and should not be bred from, since temperamental instability is certainly an inherited characteristic.

THE WORK OF THE H.I.S.

In view of the perils and pitfalls of breeding a type, rather than a specific breed, the work of the H.I.S. can be seen to be of paramount importance in Great Britain. Central to its work is the premium stallion scheme which I have mentioned. Every year the Society distributes more than £50,000 in premiums, or subsidies, to the owners of the Thoroughbred stallions selected at the annual stallion show, held in March at Newmarket. Two distinguished judges select the stallions, which are paraded at Tattersalls Park Paddocks. Conformation, action and suitability for producing quality horses with size and substance are the criteria for the judging. Racing performances of the stallions are also considered in some cases. It is a remarkable show which sorts out the basic sixty stallions which each receive a premium worth £650. At the time of the award £200 is paid and the balance follows after the close of the service season. The Society reserves the right to withhold the second part of the premium if a stallion serves less than thirty mares. The whole point of the scheme is that it endeavours to make it worthwhile for the owners of these Thoroughbred stallions to allow them to service non-Thoroughbred mares. The fee for the service of a mare owned by a member of the Society is amazingly cheap, currently a mere £38 (for non-members it is £65).

The stallions stand in designated districts, comprising one or more counties, which cover the whole of the United Kingdom. A premium stallion is required to serve mares throughout its district at the limited fee, the maximum non-Thoroughbred mares allowed in one season being eighty. The scheme does not preclude stallion owners from accepting Thoroughbred mares, and they make their own arrangements for higher fees in such cases, but it is clearly weighted in favour of the non-Thorough-bred mare. About 10% of mares covered are Thoroughbred.

At the Newmarket Show there is an important first class for young 'novice' stallions, those which have not been out of train-ing for more than two years, or have not stood at stud for more than one year, and have not previously received H.I.S. awards. The best stallion in this class receives the Macdonald-Buchanan Champion Challenge Trophy. This is followed by six classes for stallions in groups made up of the total of forty-two areas in the scheme. The horses in each class are judged and placed in order of merit, up to thirteen premiums being awarded in each class. Then comes the formidable task of finding the champion stallion in the show, who receives the King George V Challenge Cup, and a super premium of £500. The cham-pion receives £475 and there are eighteen other super premiums varying from £459 down to £100. There is a parade of all district class horses for the super premium judging, and it is fascinating to see the judges tackle this major decision-making role. Leading stallions in such crowded company is not always an easy job. It is marvellous to see the coolnesss of a handler when his stallion stands on its hind legs or kicks up its heels, with the other stallions only too close.

Being judged in a 'beauty line-up' is all very well, but the real worth of a stallion is assessed in the proportion and merit of his stock. The H.I.S. annually gives the Henry Tudor Challenge Cup for performance in the previous stud season. For example, the 1979 winner was Game Warden, who served eighty-two in the 1977–78 season and achieved a foaling percentage of 86.58. Owners of the first six award winners in this competition receive £40 cash prizes.

To give some idea of the scale of the scheme, in 1971 there were sixty-three stallions standing at stud: they served 3,860 mares, which is an average of sixty-one mares per stallion. In the 1972 foaling there were 2,295 foals; a foaling percentage of 63.86. The figures have remained reasonably constant since

The splendid foundation stock for hunter breeding: champion Irish Draught mare, Pink Carnation, owned by Mr Patrick Duane, at Dublin Show.

Henry James, by Armagnac Monarch, and owned by Sheila Willcox, overall champion of the H.I.S. National Hunter Show, 1978.

then, with 1974 seeing the highest foaling figure of 2,958. The 1977 figure was down to 2,100 foals.

I have quoted prize money and premium figures in some detail above to illustrate that it is an important financial contribution to non-Thoroughbred horse breeding in Britain, but it is of course 'small beer' compared to the millions of pounds expended on breeding the blue-blooded darlings of flat racing who are exported with increasing regularity to the blue grass of Kentucky where they stand at stud for immense fees.

At the end of June there is a marvellous opportunity to see the results of the H.I.S. activities at the National Hunter Show. The eighty-eighth of these shows was held by the Society in 1979. Fundamental to the Society's role is the maintenance of a Hunter Stud Book and nearly all prize winners in the show must be entered. The only exceptions are colts in the yearling and foal classes who would be gelded in due course, or registered later if kept as entires. There are twelve young stock classes, ranging from yearlings to three-year-olds. The emphasis is on non-Thoroughbred stock, but there are three classes in this section for Thoroughbreds. There are eight classes for brood mares and foals, two of which are specifically for full Thoroughbreds. There is also a group class of three animals by the same sire. In this show the prize money is again of a modest order, with £75 going to the winner of the championship, and £30 to the reserve champion. Prizes in the young stock classes go from £30 down to £7 for sixth place.

What does the work of the Society achieve at its present level? Its effect is invaluable, but no one would deny that it could achieve so much more with realistic financial backing. The most cynical saying in the equestrian world is that 'fools breed horses for wise men to buy'. In other words the risks, the disappointments and the sheer hard work in horse breeding are not worth the financial rewards at present obtainable.

Fortunately there is a wonderful band of people, the backbone of hunter breeding, who enjoy this activity as a way of life as much as for any commercial gain they may achieve.

This is just as well, for we in Britain are a long way yet from arriving at the enlightened state where breeders are properly rewarded by subsequent premiums or prizes when stock they have bred win races or other equestrian competitions. Attempts are being made in this direction, but they fall far short of the sort of ideal which has been expressed by the Thoroughbred Breeders' Association in terms of racing:

Success on the racecourse should be rewarded to United Kingdom breeders either directly through breeders' prizes or subsidies to mare owners, or indirectly through encouragement by additional prize money, or premiums to owners of home-bred animals.

The H.I.S. scheme has also been highly successful in producing steeplechasers. This was acknowledged by Mr John Sumner's Committee which investigated the breeding of steeplechasers on behalf of the Jockey Club and produced a most interesting report in 1978. The Committee praised the H.I.S. for its work, but the volume of steeplechasers produced under its scheme has been far short of the need if steeplechasing is not to decline. The Sumner Committee's brief was to examine the reasons why an increasing number of horses are being trained for and are competing in hurdle races at the expense of the true steeplechaser.

The main source of the H.I.S.'s income is a £50,000 grant paid by the Horserace Betting Levy Board. The levy is raised by deductions from profits made by bookmakers in Britain. The total betting turnover in Britain is £2,000 million a year; of which the Government takes over £100 million in betting tax. Income raised by the Levy Board amounts to about £9 million. This is distributed back to the racing industry in subsidies for prize money, racecourse improvements and other areas affecting racing, of which the H.I.S. is one of many.

In France racing is subsidised far more generously because bookmakers are illegal; all betting is conducted under a tote monopoly and money is distributed by the Government. French racing is awarded well over £80 million a year. There are twenty-three national studs in France, catering for every category of horse, all under the direction of the French Ministry of Agriculture. Annually they receive more than £3 million from the Ministry. A further £3,600,000 is given by the Ministry towards the encouragement of the riding horse in the form of breeders' premiums and donations towards the running of horse shows, horse trials and show jumping.

In West Germany the horse is regarded as a valuable agricultural product and the degree of government aid is indicated by the subsidies for horse breeding in one state alone, North Rhine Westphalia, of some £1,500,000 per annum.

The Irish realised the importance of the horse as a national asset and set up the Irish Horse Board. With money from the Irish government, the Horse Board spends more than £200,000 per year on breeding schemes. Stallion owners have received £73,540 in £20 subsidies for foals recorded with the Board, and foaling premiums worth £62,035 have been paid to owners of registered mares.

One of the Board's most important achievements is the establishment of the Irish Horse Register. Mares are carefully inspected before being allowed to be recorded, and up to August, 1977, the Board had accumulated some 11,600 mares on the Register and was receiving about 4,000 live foaling returns anually.

Saunter, winner for Mr Jimmy Snell of the King George V Cup in the 1978 H.I.S. Stallion Show.

The Irish and the French governments rate horses for value added tax at virtually zero; in France horses are rated for V.A.T. only at their carcase value. This is an immense advantage for breeders and dealers in competition with their counterparts in Britain where governments of both complexions have so far insisted on rating the horse at a full 15% for V.A.T.

The prospect of a tote monopoly in Britain seems increasingly remote. There was no support for the proposal by the recent Royal Commission on Betting. But a more realistic attitude by politicians towards horse breeding would be a great help. The immense contribution of the H.I.S. in improving the British riding horse is not simply a matter of economic advantages, although the horse is undoubtedly a national asset in commercial terms. Above all, it is a profound contribution to the recreational life of a country in which horse riding and driving have boomed phenomenally as leisure activities in the postwar years.

The dearest wish of the H.I.S. now is to establish the British hunter as a specific breed of riding horse instead of a type. It is vital that a strict system of registration of mares is set up if this is to be achieved. The H.I.S. maintains a Hunter Stud Book now, but no more than 300 mares register each year and registration certificates only state an animal's sire and dam. The plan is to produce a new stud book, consisting of mares and their produce based on the present Hunter Stud Book, but deleting its gelding section. All premium horses in the stud book would be registered, and their produce would only be accepted if out of registered mares. This is the crux of the new scheme.

The number of registered females would thus gradually build up into a nucleus of good mares, and after a number of years perhaps a breed of 'British hunter' could be established. In order to keep substance as well as quality in the breed, it has also been suggested that it might be possible to register another type of stallion, such as Irish Draught or similar, and then register his stock out of registered mares only.

Horse breeding is the subject of an investigation by the European Economic Community, and it is certain that a mares' register is bound to be one of the E.E.C.'s long-term requirements for all member countries. In Germany and France where such registers exist it is an immense advantage to would-be buyers to know the pedigree and background of mares as well as stallions. It is much more of a guarantee that young stock will be bred to type.

In Britain the premium stallions still have to take the non-Thoroughbred mares offered for matings, provided only that they have current veterinary certificates of health.

Germany has still not produced a real competitor to the British and Irish seven-eighths- or three-quarter-bred hunter type which has proved supremely successful in eventing. We can certainly breed good show jumpers too, but here the Germans have a growing reputation for considerable success. The Hanoverian horse has an especially good record as a show jumper, either pure bred or with outcrosses of Thoroughbred or Trakhener blood. Some British show jumpers have had immense success riding German horses in recent years. Harvey Smith and his son Robert, Ted Edgar and his wife Liz, and Caroline Bradley are among those who have done well with German-bred horses, while David Broome, the former world champion, tells me he still prefers Thoroughbreds or near T.B.

crosses, and his most successful mounts have continued to be of this stock.

FOUNDATION STOCK

It will be seen that the influence of the Thoroughbred is crucial in producing the hunter type, but the trouble with producing a type is that even considerable experts tend to have vastly different views on what that type should be. The 'mix' is the non-Thoroughbred mare, and in producing the best type of hunter with substance as well as quality, clearly the breeders' decisions made here are of enormous importance.

The Irish Draught Although its name implies that this is a horse used in harness, the Irish Draught is in fact a lighter and more agile horse than you might suppose.

In the seventeenth and eighteenth centuries more land in Ireland came under the plough. Farmers needed horses suitable

Current Magic, owned by Mr G. H. Lloyd, winner of the King George V Cup at the H.I.S. Stallion Show at Newmarket, 1979, with the trophy being presented by the President's wife, Mrs John Chamberlayne.

for heavy farm work, but the heavy war horses used by armoured knights in medieval England had not been bred in Ireland. The Irish used lighter animals as mounts for men herding sheep and cattle, and their cavalry were lightly armed and relied on speed and manoeuvring in tackling invaders.

The Irish farmers' response to the problem of the farm horse was to concentrate on breeding from their heavier native horses, and this produced a marvellously versatile animal. It could plough, draw a cart and provide a good mount for its owner. This horse came to be known as the Irish Draught. It has been defined as a deep-chested, flat-boned animal, with an oval rib cage and the shoulders of a riding horse. It has a short, smooth coat, a high-set tail and does not have the 'feather' on its heels which you find in the English heavy horse. The Irish Draught is docile and brave, and noted for its soundness and stamina.

The Draught mare put to a Thoroughbred invariably produces a wonderful hunter type. During the last war the Irish Draught continued to work on the land in Ireland, but mechanisation followed, and a great drain began on this splendid breed. Thousands were exported in boatloads for slaughter in Belgium, to provide meat for Europeans who were at the time exceedingly short of beef. Fortunately, a small band of enthusiasts kept the Irish Draught going, but it has been estimated that at one time the situation became so serious that only seventy-three Irish Draught mares were registered in one season in the early 1960s. Mr Charles Haughey, himself a hunting man, was Minister of Agriculture at the time. He realised the problem and set up a survey team to look at horse breeding, out of which grew the Irish Horse Board. Then the Greenvale Irish Draught Mare Championship was begun, with enlightened sponsorship, and this helped the revival of popularity for the breed.

The Horse Board now controls the Irish Draught Stud Book and has strict control over foals, mares and stallions. Recently a system of progeny testing and performance assessment has been introduced. The Board owns an Irish Draught Stallion, Flagmount Boy, which is being performance-tested as a show jumper.

In 1978 the number of mares in the stud book rose to 1,246;

the number covered by Irish Draught sires was 320, and the live foals registered amounted to 176. In that year there were sixty-two Irish Draught sires standing at stud in Ireland, and all their lists were filled.

Early in 1979 the British Irish Draught Horse Society was formed by English enthusiasts. They listed ten Irish Draught stallions standing at stud in England for the 1979 season.

The Irish Draught stallion may be bred to a Thoroughbred mare, of course, but for a combination of substance, bone and quality the Irish Draught mare crossed with a Thoroughbred stallion is a better bet.

Cleveland Bay This breed has long been regarded as an ideal foundation stock for the hunter type when crossed with Thoroughbred blood. The Cleveland Bay has been recognised as a distinct breed for more than 200 years, originating in North Yorkshire as a ride and drive animal on the farms. It could take its turn at the plough, but could also take the family on outings in a gig. It should be a bay colour with black points, and no white other than a small star: the height is 16 to 16.2 hands; and the animal should have 215–240 mm ($8\frac{1}{2}$–$9\frac{1}{2}$ in) of flat bone below the knee, and no long hairs on the legs. It should be a short-legged horse, with good feet. The breed is noted for its equable temperament.

As a carriage horse, the pure Cleveland Bay has been criticised for being somewhat slow, and in the fast-growing sport of combined driving, where time is all important, the teams-of-four turnouts prefer to use Oldenburgs and other Continental breeds. Nevertheless, Cleveland Bay blood at the first or second cross certainly produces excellent riding horses. In fact, the breed's widespread use as foundation stock nearly endangered the survival of the pure Cleveland Bay. Much was done to assist its recent revival when Col Sir John Miller, the Crown Equerry, bought for the Queen the stallion Mulgrave Supreme, bred in 1961, and at the time of writing standing successfully at Mr Max Abram's stud near Westow, North Yorkshire. In 1977 the Queen visited the Great Yorkshire Show when her now famous stallion paraded with a remarkable collection of his progeny.

Hilly Leys, by Mibus, belonging to Mr Peter Hobbs, won the Edward Prince of Wales Cup for the champion young horse at the H.I.S. National Hunter Show at Shrewsbury, 1979.

Arabs As we have seen, the Arab horse is the original foundation stock for the Thoroughbred, but thanks to its devoted admirers throughout the world it retains its status as one of the most important breeds in its own right. I have included it in my list of foundation stock for the hunter, rather than as the ideal means of achieving the 'hunter type', which would be a larger horse of more substance.

The Anglo-Arab, a cross between an Arab and a Thoroughbred, has proved itself a superb cross-country animal. As a practical hunter for the light man, most women, and teenagers, an Anglo-Arab can be ideal.

Arabs crossed with native ponies are renowned for their success in producing good quality riding ponies, and the Arab influence on Connemaras, Welsh ponies and cobs, and the New Forest breed, can be particularly successful. A good Arab stallion bequeathes quality, stamina, and hardiness to his stock.

The Shire and other heavy horses The Shire, the Suffolk Punch and other heavy horses may well have been the foundation stock used some generations back for many a hunter, or even a show hunter type. In an attempt to get back to the really 'big sort', experiments are currently being made in putting Shire mares to T.B. stallions, and even vice versa, but it is too early to say whether these have had any real success.

It is tempting to reject the idea out of hand because of the risk of losing quality purely at the expense of gaining in size. The aim of one breeder engaging in this cross was ultimately to produce show jumpers where speed might be said to matter less than strength and jumping ability. I am inclined to doubt the feasibility of this policy, even for show jumping where the international honours still seem to go to German-bred horses, Thoroughbreds, or near Thoroughbreds. The modern emphasis on fast jumping off against the clock makes sheer speed an asset in nearly every competition nowadays.

Part-bred stock By far the largest percentage of mares put to Thoroughbred stallions to produce the 'hunter type' are not, in fact, pure-bred examples of the breeds mentioned so far in this chapter. They are mares which are themselves half- or three-quarter-bred, and in Britain are more often than not of 'breeding unknown'. As I have explained, it is hoped to redress this situation, with a proper register of mares and records of their breeding being kept. Until then, much is dependent on the wisdom of individual breeders in selecting and using the best mares to produce the right type. Newcomers to breeding whose experience of equestrianism is limited should not hesitate to seek advice before putting that 'favourite old mare' to stud. Why contribute to the great pool of mediocre horses without much future when with a little more trouble you could produce something so much better? Certainly the H.I.S. scheme offers the newcomer to hunter breeding the best value for money, in terms of advice as well as selectivity of stallions for extremely reasonable stud fees. For a modest annual subscription an H.I.S. member gets free admission to the Thoroughbred Stallion Show, the National Hunter Show, and to the grand-stand of the Royal Show where the H.I.S. ridden hunter classes are judged. As described above, members are eligible to use the premium stallion scheme at specially reduced fees. Additionally, the H.I.S. runs a scheme for mares owned by members at selected affiliated shows, offering a £15 premium to mares which have produced foals in the current calendar by premium stallions. Furthermore, there are H.I.S. sales of stock sired by premium stallions which I shall describe in more detail later.

THE FUTURE

The H.I.S. can be criticised for the limitations of its current schemes, but these are due solely to a lack of financial resources, not to a lack of dedicated voluntary work.

Those of us who have long advocated a tote monopoly are not likely to see that dream realised for a long time, if ever. British politicians seem far too wedded to the needs of the bookmaking fraternity to grasp the nettle of 'nationalising' betting on horseracing, despite its manifest benefits abroad. Mr Woodrow Wyatt has done a superb job recently in vitalising and expanding the tote in Britain, and he has called for the speedy implementation of at least an off-course tote monopoly to reap greater rewards for the racing industry, and this would undoubtedly help the breeding work of the H.I.S.

The Sumner Committee report recognised the importance of the H.I.S. when it firmly recommended that any promotional scheme for improvement in the breeding of steeplechasers should incorporate, where possible, the H.I.S. scheme. I understand it would cost the H.I.S. something in excess of £10,000 per year to get its proposed register of brood mares established and working. This is not a great deal of money compared with the vast sums spent on the sponsorship of races and other equestrian events. Show jumping alone receives more than $£\frac{1}{2}$ million per annum from sponsors. It is difficult to persuade commercial firms to give money to promotional schemes which appear to earn them little in terms of immediate widespread publicity. Yet so many ancillary firms are now making good profits indirectly from the horse that I hope the time will come for a concerted effort by the equestrian trade to contribute jointly to safeguard the hunter type.

CHAPTER 4

The Cob

AN EXPERIENCED horseman knows a cob when he sees one, but he cannot describe a guaranteed method of breeding one. The true cob is something of a freak. The Welsh Cob is a well-defined breed, but the term 'cob' applied to other animals refers to a type. People will speak disparagingly of a horse being 'a bit cobby', the the same critics will enthuse when they see what they will tell you is a 'real cob'.

As a working hunter a good cob takes some beating, but his scope will not encompass country such as Leicestershire, where sheer galloping is still required. This does not mean that you could not have a splendid day on a cob in the Shires, but that you should not expect to be in the 'front seat in the stalls' throughout the programme. However, since a great many people never really aspire to be in that position, and cannot get there, nor stay there, on expensive horseflesh, I often reflect that some of them would be a lot better off on confidential cobs which can really jump well and will stand up to the rough and tumble of the hunting field better than some weedy types which may be ridden with singular lack of success.

How do you breed a cob? It is undoubtedly a by-product of hunter breeding, that is by putting half-bred or part-bred mares to Thoroughbred stallions, or heavy horse stallions to Thoroughbred or Arab mares. From this cross a proportion of short-legged horses with pony-like heads and necks will be produced.

At one time cobs were invariably docked to show off their fine, powerful quarters. Nowadays docking is illegal, and the British Show Hack and Cob Association specifies that only undocked cobs may be shown. The height limit for the show cob is 15.1 hands, but on the question of weights there has been

At the International Horse Show, held at the White City Stadium in London, in 1948: weight carrying cob Knobby, ridden and exhibited by Mrs R. Cooke. Making the presentation is Col the Hon Guy Cubitt, who became Life President of the Pony Club.

A great show man, Mr Roy Trigg, with the winning weight carrying cob Jonathan, owned by Miss Baldry, at the Royal Show.

some recent controversy, which is typical of the problems associated with a type rather than a breed. The old conception of the animal was purely as a heavyweight. Before the name cob was used the type was called a 'rouncy', derived from the French *roncin* and the Latin *runcinus*, and in feudal times was ridden by a squire in war and by his reeve, or estate steward, in peace. Recently a number of enthusiasts have pressed the case for more shows to include classes for lightweight as well as heavyweight cobs, and there was some argument as to whether the class should divide at 86 kilos (13 stone 7 lb), or 90 kilos (14 stone).

Currently it remains at 86 kilos (13 stone 7 lb). In most cases the judges have the option of deciding whether or not to divide the class, depending on the size and numbers of entries. In 1979 about fourteen shows with qualifiers for the Horse of the Year Show decided to divide their classes into lightweight and heavyweight, with the champion and reserve going on to Wembley where there is just one heavyweight class. In recent years we have such wonderful Wembley champions as Kempley and Cromwell, beautifully shown by Robert Oliver, and the

splendid Jonathan, the grey which won the Cob of the Year title four times.

The best sort of cob displays a great depth through the girth, has a wonderfully kind eye, and looks as if he could go on all day, with safety if not with the greatest speed, although it has to be conceded that the really good show cobs do move remarkably well.

The Welsh Cob is known as Section D of the Welsh Pony breed. It came originally from Cardiganshire and Pembrokeshire, and stands between 13.2 h.h. and 15 h.h. Welsh Cobs are noted for their good constitution, hard flinty bone, courage, activity and equable temperament. They are strong enough to carry a man, but should be quiet enough to be a safe ride for a young girl.

The cob's great appeal nowadays must surely be its usefulness as a genuine ride and drive animals. They will usually perform splendidly in harness, and indeed Mr George Bowman has proved that you can win international combined driving three-day events with teams of four Welsh Cobs. The cob earns his place in a study of the hunter because at his best he is an excellent performer in the hunting field, although as I have indicated he has his limitations.

I had an Irish-bred cob, called Ballyn Garry, for about ten seasons. He never hunted in Leicestershire, but he did carry me in more than twenty-five different hunting countries elsewhere and always performed superbly. Although being somewhat above show height, about 15.3 h.h., he was a real cob type, but he had rather too high a knee action to be accounted a brilliant mover under saddle. He was a fabulous ride in the hunting field; he never turned his head, and he soared over any type of obstacle with enormous boldness and surprising scope. Although I am tall and long-legged, I never felt under-horsed with him. I bought him in Surrey and used to hunt him with the Old Surrey and Burstow and the Mid-Surrey Farmers' Drag in the days when the Hon. Philip Kindersley gave a daunting lead over enormous fences. Garry used to take on anything boldly, provided one had the nerve to give him his head. I took him down to Dorset later, and was rather worried as to whether he would manage the deep going, big hedges and

Superb example of a Welsh cob: Llanarth Stud's Llanarth Flying Comet, winner of the Lloyds Bank In-Hand Championship at the 1979 Horse of the Year Show.

A distinguished National Pony Show winner, Welsh cob Turkdean Cerdin, winner of the Shalbourne Challenge Cup for the best Mountain and Moorland Pony Stallion. Note the compact strength of this useful cob; up to weight and with considerable endurance.

drops and wide ditches of the vale country. He not only managed them, but clearly enjoyed the challenge and gave me some of my happiest hunting there.

I have included this personal reminiscence as a testimony to the qualities of a cob. Good ones have been in somewhat short supply in recent years, and I hope very much that recent signs of a revival will escalate to result in the production of many more. Although it is impossible to guarantee breeding the true cob type, breeders would obviously take more chances in aiming for a 'cobby' animal if they knew there was an eager market.

The modern emphasis on 'quality' and the increasing numbers of comparatively lightweight girls and women in all the competitive riding sports has made the production of the weight-carrier a much less attractive breeding prospect. This may be offset now by the current boom in the ride and drive animal, and the 'true cob' should benefit.

CHAPTER 5

The Hunter Pony and the Arab Horse

ONE OF my favourite cartoons was drawn by Leech in the last century. It shows a venerable, bearded hunting man pounding up a slope, next to a little boy on a diminutive pony. 'You had better take a pull uphill if you want to save your pony,' warns the old man.

'Mind you own business,' replies the child. 'There's my man over there with my second horse,' pointing to a groom standing by a gateway with another tiny pony.

The fact is that a good pony can perform prodigiously in the hunting field, and is hardly likely to need the aid of a 'second horse' no matter how many hills it has to ascend. Children in the British Isles are fortunate in having so many breeds of native ponies, most of which make superb riding animals and can be used to follow hounds effectively and safely. Soundness and stamina are essential in any form of hunter, as we have already emphasised. The pony of native stock, or one with a large degree of native blood, is usually faultless in this respect.

I should point out that in many parts of the country ponies make ideal hunters for adults as well as children. The main factor in choosing a pony for a child to hunt is not so much the finer points of its conformation as its temperament. Few children are likely to enjoy being launched into the hunting field on ponies which are too hot and cannot be held, but this is a generalisation, and I am constantly amazed by the ability of some very young children to manage high-spirited animals. In the main, however, it is particularly important that the hunter pony has good manners. The little devils can have a strong tendency to kick each other, and horses – and hounds. This needs checking right at the start, and I blame the parents of children whose ponies misbehave in this way.

72

A badly behaved pony can be just as dangerous to other people's lives and limbs as to the child on its back. On far too many occasions I have been approaching a fence at speed when a pony has dived in from the side on a collision course. More than once my horse has jumped the hindquarters of the pony as well as the fence.

Children need every encouragement to hunt, and there is nothing I hate more than to hear them being shouted at in the hunting field, but too often it is the fault of their parents, who have sent them out on unschooled, or badly schooled ponies. Ponies with strong tendencies to lie down in mud or water, or just anywhere, and those which snatch at the bit and suddenly put their heads down to graze, are beyond the pale as good hunters.

I should now declare that for every rogue, there are many more superb hunter ponies, and it just needs a little care and

One of the best native ponies for the hunting field – and a great foundation stock when crossed with Thoroughbreds: the Connemara. Mrs J. Williams's Cocum Hawkstone, five-year-old stallion, won the Championship at the English Connemara Pony Society Show.

At the Arabian performance show, the Countess of Pembroke, hostess for the show at Wilton Park, competes in the bending race with her stallion, Sunlight's Allegro.

the right advice for parents to find mounts which will afford their children hours of fun in the hunting field, and teach them more than any expensive riding instructor.

David Broome, the former world champion show jumper, and one of the greatest natural horsemen in the world, ascribes much of his success in acquiring a firm seat and good hands to his early experience in the hunting field in the Curre country on a family pony. He is now Joint Master of the Curre.

One can see ponies excelling themselves as hunters in many

areas, especially the moorland countries where they are in their natural habitat and display a sure-footedness and agility well beyond most horses. On Exmoor one used to see shepherds mounted on native ponies following the staghounds more successfully than other followers on large blood hunters.

I was fortunate in riding New Forest ponies as a boy. We used to buy them unbroken at the annual Beaulieu Road pony

Mrs McMillen riding Dadia by Darjeel, winner of the Arab class at the 1976 Royal International Horse Show. Arabs and Arab-cross animals are frequently seen in the hunting field nowadays.

sales for very little money just after the war; one of the best I had cost fourteen guineas. The New Forest is a comparatively easy breed to break and school, and they are hardy and particularly suitable for the taller child, being up to 14.2 h.h. Their narrowness of conformation is also a boon for the child rider. They make an excellent cross with Arab or Thoroughbred blood for the teenager, but do not forget that you are increasing the likelihood of producing a far more ebullient pony which may take a lot more riding.

The child's first pony may be taken on a leading rein to the meet, or possibly stand about at the covert side during cub-hunting. This is excellent as a 'familiarisation process' for the child, but the real hunter pony must carry its young charge across country safely and comfortably, and I firmly believe that the good native pony has a larger share of common sense in performing this task than many cross-bred animals.

A good hunter pony should take all sorts of strange noises and sights without violent reaction; in particular, he must be absolutely perfect in traffic, and here the New Forest is often especially good. This is not because the ponies you see grazing in the Forest become accustomed to the traffic speeding past them. Even with modern fencing, far too many of these ponies are killed on the roads. No, it is a matter of temperament, and in any case, I would advise a parent looking for a good example of a New Forest pony to try some of the studs specialising in the breed before thinking of buying 'off the Forest'. The stud-reared pony will have had a better chance to grow and develop properly as a foal. Conditions in the Forest itself are not always ideal nowadays. Far too many ponies die of malnutrition in a severe winter, and there are undoubted problems of redworm infestation and overgrazing in some areas.

On Dartmoor, the ponies you see grazing among the heather are almost certainly not ponies of the Dartmoor breed, but scrub ponies turned out by local people, and all too often sold for the meat market. The Dartmoor Pony Breed Society is particularly active and enthusiastic, and you can find Dartmoor studs in many parts of the country. These ponies are up to 12.2 h.h., and are usually bay, black or brown. The more handling they get as young stock the better. Their sure-footedness is remarkable, although having hunted on Dartmoor's granite-strewn moors I am not surprised that its native pony has developed this facility to such a high degree. Galloping downhill over this treacherous terrain on a large horse I would have given quite a lot to be small enough to ride a native pony.

On Exmoor you will see a small number of pure Exmoor ponies grazing on the open moor; they are members of the Anchor herd and their breeding goes back into prehistory. It is claimed the Exmoor has been recognisable as a distinct breed as far back as the Bronze Age, and they were later said to be the chariot horses of the Celts.

Exmoors have characteristic mealy-coloured noses, a mealy ring round the eye, known as a 'toad eye', and a fan-like growth at the top of the tail, called an 'ice tail'. Again, they can make good hunter ponies, but it should be said – even at the risk of upsetting Exmoor enthusiasts – that they can be particularly 'high-couraged' little animals and need plenty of handling when young, and careful breaking, to ensure that they are a tractable ride. In moorland countries they are superb, and their stamina and toughness make them particularly suitable as economical members of the equine 'family circle'. Their height should not exceed 12.2 h.h. in mares, and 12.3 h.h. in stallions.

The range and adaptability of the Welsh pony is justifiably renowned. I have referred to Section D of the stud book, the Welsh Cob; its smaller brother is Section C, the Welsh Pony of Cob Type which stands between 12 and 13.2 h.h. These smaller cobs come from Breconshire and Radnorshire, and are good ride and drive animals.

Section B comprises ponies of splendid riding type up to 13.2 h.h., and they usually make particularly good hunters for children, being excellent performers in a grass vale country as well as rougher hill terrains. The Welsh Mountain pony forms Section A, standing up to 12 h.h., and a delightful animal it is, with much brightness about its outlook and performance.

Declaring my own personal preference as to a hunter pony, I must opt for the Connemara. They are from 13 to 14.2 h.h. and can make marvellous mounts for adults as well as children. It has been said that horses rescued from wrecked ships of the Spanish Armada on the Irish coast in 1588 became absorbed in the breed. Certainly there is a suggestion of Spanish or Arab blood, which is allied with the sturdy qualities of a basic native Irish breed. Connemaras tend to have especially nice temperaments and their conformation should include good sloping shoulders and well-balanced heads and necks.

I always marvel at the performance of ponies in the Irish hunting field, and at the skill and bravery of the children who ride them. They will tackle the huge double banks of Limerick without a tremor, leaping on to the sheer face of a bank across a yawning ditch, shinning up its surface to the top, and then leaping safely down the other side. These banks are 1.5 to 3 metres (5 to 10 ft) high, with thick growth on them. Similarly, these ponies will launch themselves over enormous ditches, and jump or bank craggy, crumbling walls. They will also leap sticks in gaps with wonderful natural agility. I have seen a Connemara pony fall into a deep ditch and fronds of growth close over the heads of pony and child rider. Suddenly there was a scrabbling noise and they both emerged together like a cork from a bottle and galloped off none the worse! Some of the best Irish horses and cobs in the hunting field have considerable elements of Connemara blood in them. It is marvellous as foundation stock, as well as a pure breed.

A Connemara breed show supreme champion, Miss Pat Lyne's Arctic Moon.

I have described the above-mentioned native breeds as ideal sources of pure-bred hunter ponies, and the great benefit of buying one is that you have a much better idea of what you are getting, and you may also have the satisfaction of showing the pony in the native classes, or later on breeding from a mare. However, the vast majority of hunter ponies are just 'utility ponies', of course, and may have varying degrees of different native blood, which could just as easily include Dales, Fell, Highland, or Shetland. The versatility of the pony is such that all the native breeds can provide conveyance under saddle across country, but the latter-mentioned breeds have much stronger traditions as pack or harness animals.

The Arab enthusiast will not really approve of my tacking on a reference to this renowned breed at the end of a chapter on ponies, for the Arab is a horse, not a pony. I have already paid tribute to its immense influence as a foundation for the modern Thoroughbred, and to its continued importance as a sire to produce quality stock from so many other breeds, including native ponies. Enthusiasts also extol the pure-bred Arab as a hunter. This is a claim which I have heard hotly disputed, but as I have never hunted a pure-bred Arab I cannot bear personal witness. Nevertheless, I am perfectly willing to accept that the Arab can perform remarkably well in the hunting field; indeed I have seen some members of the breed doing so. They would suit lighter men and women, and teenagers, and I am not sure that I would want to ride them in big, scopey country – although some people will hotly disagree with this view.

I am much impressed by the Arab's ability to travel long distances with remarkable displays of stamina and basic soundness. This was demonstrated in the 1979 Golden Horseshoe long distance ride on Exmoor when the horses had to contend with a heatwave during the first day's 80-kilometre (50-mile) ride, and then much colder conditions with mist over 40 kilometres (25 miles) on the second day. Arab horses acquitted themselves well, and there was a high proportion of them among the twenty finishers out of sixty-four starters.

Speed is a valuable asset in a hunter, too, and the Arab is certainly fleet. In Britain the Arab Horse Society runs regular races for Arab horses with the approval of the Jockey Club.

CHAPTER 6

Hunters in the Hunting Field

> . . . and if I was a'going to ride for my life
> tomorrow over a country I'd never seen before, I'd
> ask for a four-year-old to do it on.
>
> *G. J. Whyte-Melville.*

LOOKING AT hunters in the show ring or the sale yard is great
fun, and an invitation to inspect someone's hunting stable is
always a treat. The groom, or more often nowadays the proud
owner himself, takes off the rugs for each horse to be inspected.
You make appreciative remarks, and mentally you note the
horse in the stable you would like to take home.

How would he carry me? This is the crucial question every
horseman asks himself in buying a horse for the hunting field.
For the follower who hunts solely for his own pleasure, the
choice of the right horse is vital. Riding a really bad horse
usually spoils your day's hunting, no matter how much you
adore watching hounds, being out in the countryside, or taking
the opportunity to inspect the standard of farming of your
friends and neighbours.

'Going well' requires an eye for the country, quick reflexes,
and the essential skills of presenting a horse properly at the
best place in a fence at the right pace. Yet above all, the man or
woman who consistently goes well – as I have observed rather
than practised – is the rider who unfailingly follows the old
axiom: 'Throw your heart over the fence first.'

The invisible thread of confidence between a rider and horse
is an unmistakable part of the bond which produces an effective combination across country. It is the factor which enables
one man to get the best out of a moderate horse; it is the reason
why a good horse can be so quickly spoilt by a poor rider in the
hunting field.

The worst, and alas the most frequent, fault of the poor

rider is bad hands; all too often you see people chopping horses in the mouth when jumping. A good brave horse will put up with this for a surprisingly long time; but the pain and shock of being caught in the mouth when he extends his neck to jump a big fence usually stops him eventually. His relish for jumping is killed; he associates it with discomfort and even pain, and the bold carefree jumper bought for a high price quickly becomes a sulky refuser.

Bad hands are probably born of a lack of confidence; often an unconscious default, for the rider may have plenty of courage, but never have acquired a safe seat in all circumstances, never have learned to sit securely when jumping, and thus unknowingly have acquired the habit of hanging on to the reins and jabbing his horse in the mouth at crucial moments.

Amazingly, some horses accommodate to this cruel defect simply by developing iron-hard mouths, seizing the bit and taking charge at every fence. Hence, the growing number of 'unstoppable' horses. Every bit is tried without success, and

High quality hunters out with the Quorn Hunt; beautifully turned out, but with unplaited manes, which is frequently seen in Leicestershire.

December snow does not deter this hunter, going well with Mr James Teacher, Joint Master of the Quorn, in a run in the famous Friday country.

although a heavy, strong man may achieve a considerable amount of brake power by sheer strength, a lighter rider can have recorse only to such drastic measures as the gag bit.

There have probably never been so many gag bits in the hunting field as you will see nowadays, and I am not totally condemning their use. The gag bit is delightfully simple: the

One of Leicestershire's most popular personalities, Mrs Ulrica Murray Smith, Joint Master of the Quorn since 1959. Her hunter is standing quietly but paying close attention as hounds draw the Prince of Wales covert.

rein and cheek piece are not attached separately to the ring of the bit, as in a snaffle; instead, the rein is joined to the cheek piece by means of a slim piece of leather which slides up or down through two holes, one at the top and the other at the bottom of the bit ring. This exercises enormous leverage when the rider pulls the rein. It causes the leather cheek extension to slip down across the ring, pulling on the cheek piece which is attached to the headband of the bridle, and thus using as a lever the top of the horse's head, which produces tremendous power in dragging the bit back across the bars of the horse's mouth. Some people also use a top rein attached to the rings of this bit, which acts as an ordinary snaffle, only picking up the lower rein to act as a gag when extra leverage on the mouth is required. This is preferable, but I detect an increasing tendency to rely on the gag rein alone.

Using a gag effectively requires hands well above average. An untimely jab in the mouth with a snaffle is bad enough, but with a gag bit it can be a real stopper. The danger in riding natural country is the unexpected hazard, which can cause even the best of riders a moment of unbalance and a loss of grip, when it is all too easy to hang on to the reins. The sad fact is that bad hands cause the horse to develop a hard mouth, which leads to the use of increasingly severe bits, ending in the employment of the gag by a rider whose hands started the trouble; a vicious circle indeed.

The solution is better breaking and schooling of hunters in the first place. Most of the old nagsmen have gone; there has been an explosion of riding in the postwar years, and the availability of adequate riding tuition to meet the needs of people who did not grow up in a horsy background is far short of the requirement.

Apart from a shortage of riding instruction, there is an even more significant dearth of top-class teaching in the art of breaking young horses properly. Modern economics also allow for less time between the basic breaking of a horse and its appearance on the market as a 'made' hunter. You will often hear hunting people extol the virtues of a hunter which has 'done a bit of show jumping', or 'been eventing now and again'. I am sure the reason why such horses often make excellent hunters is not merely that they have competed, but that they have had more groundwork and basic schooling than a great many hunters who have been taught only by going 'through the mill'. How can you look after your horse in the hunting field while reaping the maximum reward for all the money and time spent in acquiring and keeping the brute?

There was a time when it was the custom rather than the exception for hunts to buy cobs especially for use during the cubhunting season. Some individuals did the same, but this is a comparatively rare procedure nowadays, for economic reasons. The advantages are that your good hunters are spared the rigours of long autumn mornings when all too often the ground is hard and tendons can receive punishment before the real season begins. 'It's only cubhunting' is a foolish, but too often heard description of the activities required of a horse before 1st November. Those early morning meets and a return to the stable at lunchtime, or even later, mean that your horse is out working for five, six or even more hours. It is still worth while for hunts, therefore, to provide ponies or cobs for hunt staffs where possible during cubhunting, but the individual follower using the horse he intends to hunt throughout the season must adopt some sensible precautions.

In my chapter on hunter care I have described the vital need for slow work before horses enter the hunting field each season. Horses vary enormously in the amount of time and slow work they need to get fit, but with any horse it is a mistake to endeavour to get him fit actually in the field during cubhunting. You may get away with it for a season or two, but you are taking serious risks in shortening the working life of your hunter, and if he is a good one he will be hard to replace nowadays at any price. Much better to get him reasonably fit in slow road work *before* you go cubhunting.

The value of cubhunting is in improving your horse's manners. When hounds are put into covert in those first early morning excursions, make sure your horse stands quietly and sensibly at the covert-side. Do not tolerate a horse's attempts to fool about right at the start of the season; it will be increasingly difficult to instil manners later on if you allow your young, green horse to get away with a lot of nonsense during cubhunting. It is extremely good for him to learn to leave other horses and proceed at a sedate pace round the covert-side to take up a station in assisting the 'holding up' of the covert while hounds draw. Similarly, when it is time to move on to another covert, do not allow your horse to dash off in an uncontrolled manner. Make him wait until you are ready to join the other horses, and if he is young it will do him good at this stage in his education to keep him at or near the back.

Although cubhunting may be useful in improving your horse's general behaviour, it is not the time or the place for a showdown with a recalcitrant rogue. That situation, if you are unlucky enough to experience it, should have occurred at home before you bring your new horse out in public.

The real priority of cubhunting is to train the young hounds and you are only at the covert-side at the Master's invitation, not by right as a subscriber. You will be a danger to yourself and others if your horse is far too gassy to be allowed out in company. If you suspect that your horse is at all likely to kick then he must be kept well away from other horses, and certainly away from hounds. The very first time he kicks at anything he must be severely chastised with whip and voice immediately so that he can relate the punishment to the crime. The pain, not to say anguish, of being kicked on the leg by someone else's horse in the hunting field is inflamed even more when the rider says helplessly: 'I can't think why he did it. He's never done it before . . .'.

The answer is: 'Well thrash him immediately, and perhaps he will never do it again.'

As cubhunting progresses there will be an increasing tendency to get short sharp runs out of covert, with perhaps some jumping if you are in a country where fences abound. Be sensible in the degree to which you take part in this; the vital factors are the fitness of your horse and the state of the ground. I am by no means being a spoil-sport, as I know what tremendous fun such runs can be during cubhunting, but what a pity it is to ruin the horse you had hoped to hunt for the rest of the season.

The fitness of your horse at this stage is a vital factor in deciding when to go to home. It is not so much the intensity of the work which may drag down his condition, it is the long hours out of the stable at a time when he is still making the immense transition from an animal grazing on grass to being artificially kept indoors, clipped, and fed on corn, bran and hay, or some substitute feed. Big horses are especially prone to problems due to being rushed into hard work before they are really fit, and these are the animals which particularly benefit from slow road work instead of being alternately galloped about or kept standing during cubhunting.

Hopefully you will have got your horse really fit in time for the October cubhunting when many packs do quite a lot of work in the open, and very enjoyable such hunting can be. With the modern hunting season tending to be curtailed so much earlier in the spring due to modern farming's cultivation schedules, it is all the more worthwhile to ensure that you get as much sport as possible earlier in the season.

Cubhunting is the time to discover whether your new horse really is good to box. A horse which will not walk up the ramp of a trailer or horse box without a lot of trouble is infuriating, and this is especially the case with a hunter.

The modern hunter must rely on a horse box or trailer to arrive safely at most meets. Fortunately the majority of horses actually learn to associate the vehicle with food, warmth and a trip home to the comfort of the stable. I have often detected my mount pricking his ears when he nears his own horse box, and practically knocking me down in his eagerness to get up the ramp.

The use of two horses in a day's hunting persists in the shires and other Midlands areas. Elsewhere it is mainly huntsmen, whippers-in and sometimes Field Masters who are fortunate enough to have two a day. Two horses are always better than one, in my opinion. It is, as I have already remarked in relation to cubhunting, the length of time out of the stable which really tires the big horse, and which causes aggravation of leg or foot problems. Muscles get weary during a long day, especially in deep going, and it is then that a horse may not be using his limbs effectively, and sprains and other stresses may occur.

In Leicestershire the leading packs still organise on their fixture cards a special point for second horses during a day's hunting. No longer do you see the support army of second horsemen following the hunt on the roads, as you did up to the last war. Instead, the boxes which brought the first horses to the meet return to their stables to pick up the second horses which are trundled to the next stopping place where, in due course, they are exchanged for the first horses. Yet another

The Quorn hounds move from a meet near Lowesby. First whipper-in Tony Wright is in front, with huntsman Michael Farrin following with hounds.

rendezvous may be arranged to pick up the second horses at the end of the day.

It is an expensive and time-consuming business, expecially as some livery stables even arrange to move their clients' cars from the meet to the final pick-up spot. Luxury hunting indeed, but a great boon to the busy businessman who can only rush to the hunting field for a snatched day's hunting in the midst of a hectic work schedule.

Assuming you have loaded your horse successfully, it is to be hoped that you already have a firm idea as to where you are going to park. Nothing spoils the day more than a horse box stuck in a muddy lane, or a trailer bogged down on a verge which proved much softer than you thought!

Organisation is the key to good hunting, in the words of that great Master and huntsman, Capt Ronnie Wallace, and this applies to individuals just as much as to the hunt itself. Do try to give yourself time to get your horse out of the vehicle in an unhurried manner. You will have driven to the meet with your horse wearing a day rug and a tail bandage to avoid the rubbing *en route* which inevitably occurs otherwise. You should also have with you a sweat sheet for the return journey, and if the journey is as long as an hour you should have brought a partly filled haynet for your mount to munch on the way home. It must be kept out of his way on the outward journey, of course, as you do not want him to gallop virtually in the middle of a meal.

I much prefer taking horses to the meet fully tacked up, with a head collar over the bridle. It means the saddle is warm and comfortable before you mount the animal at the roadside; an important point on a frosty morning!

If you are fortunate enough to be accompanied, all is well, but it is not easy on your own to unload a fit hunter, take off his surcingle and tail bandage, tighten his girth, check his curb chain and throat lash, and put up the ramp again with the horse dancing about impatiently. The you have to grope in the Land Rover or horse box cab for your own top hat or other headgear, plus gloves, whip, and perhaps a flask and field money. I have suffered every sort of disaster in doing this, including losing the horse, which galloped off to the meet on his own, leaving a forlorn figure stumping along the road in hunting boots until a kindly soul brought back the scoundrel.

The best way is to work out a plan in your own mind, and stick to it in an orderly manner. Otherwise you will at last get mounted and then find you have left your spurs locked up in the Land Rover, or arrive at the meet with a tail bandage still on; someone will take much delight in pointing this out pretty quickly. More than once I have hunted all day with a tail bandage bulging in my breeches pocket.

A hunting crop, or more correctly a hunting whip, is not an ornament but an essential piece of equipment in the hunting field. The crooked end is vital in opening gates quickly, and also serves to fend off swinging gates as you go through in procession. The lash really is essential if you are to minimise the risk of your horse, or other horses, kicking a hound, Just hold the lash out at arm's length – do not crack it – when hounds pass close to your horse and they will steer clear of it, and your horse. Cracking your whip is permissible when you are standing round a covert during cubhunting and wish to assist in heading back the fox. Personally, I am not madly keen on rigorous

holding up of coverts, but it depends on the Master's wishes and the priority of culling the local fox population.

When you arrive at the meet on your hunter, having hacked sedately from your box, do not immediately forget your equine partner in the euphoria of meeting your friends. You will have parked at least 800 metres (half a mile) away from the meet because it is good manners and avoids cluttering the surrounding area, and because it will do your horse good to settle down before the dramas of encountering other horses and hounds, not to mention people on foot who may unwittingly cause him more alarm than anything else by waving at him, or poking umbrellas in his direction. Some will blithely push infants in prams virtually under his lethal, metal-shod feet.

By all means partake of the stirrup cup which may be offered you, but if you are riding a new horse beware of trouble. I have a mare called Josephine who nearly always shies at a tray of drinks, then gives a little buck or a lurch just as I am about to raise the glass to my lips. I have a remarkable collection of port-stained hunting ties.

Chat to your friends at the meet, but keep a wary eye all the time for the other horse which looks like kicking, and do not

One of the most famous settings in the world of foxhunting – in front of Badminton House, as the Duke of Beaufort's hounds move off, with huntsman Brian Gupwell. It was the opening meet, 1978.

allow your horse to get into a situation where he could all too easily kick or be kicked.

Your first priority at the meet should have been to say good morning to the Master, doffing your hat if, in the modern jargon of equal opportunities, you are 'a male hunting person'. From then on you must concentrate, and keep your eyes on the hounds, the huntsman and the Field Master. Hopefully you will not be one of those still coffee-housing and lounging about when the Master requests the huntsman to take the hounds away from the meet. You will be ready, with your horse's head pointed towards the pack as they pass you, and you will fall into rank in the procession following the Field Master. If you have come out to hunt, rather than to school your horse at the back, or fiddle about aimlessly, then I strongly advise you to take a good position right from the start. There is no need to be ill-mannered about it, but quick decision-making is the art of following hounds on a horse, and there is much to be said for getting near the action immediately.

One of the worst experiences is to keep catching up the leaders who have paused while hounds check briefly. You join them on a blowing horse, and immediately they are off again, giving your mount no respite if you are to stay with them. But I am running away from my attempt to describe each stage of a hunt for the mounted follower who seeks to enjoy himself to the full in a real partnership with his horse. Having, then, secured your position reasonably near the front as hounds trot up the road, try to keep in touch with the leaders in the mounted field when they leave the tarmac, but do endeavour not to let your horse career about as soon as he gets his feet on to grass. By all means follow the Field Master at the same pace if he canters to a position near the first covert to be drawn, but do not gallop wildly alongside him. From the start, ride your horse as if you intend to control him independently; do not let him adopt a sheep-like attitude and follow the flock all day. I am well aware that more than a few hunting people follow hounds in this manner all their seasons in the hunting field. They are not the ones, however, who are capable of turning their horses' heads away from the crowd on occasions and taking their own line over a feasible fence which enables them to ride *to* hounds instead of constantly following the back of the man in front.

The Field Master, if he knows his business, will have made the mounted field halt in a position where they can easily catch up when hounds leave the covert, but where the horses are not going to head a fox should he go away.

I will assume that you are fortunate and hounds find in the first covert. A whipper-in posted at the far end raises his hat and screeches a holloa or in some (scientific) hunting countries he will blow a whistle instead. The huntsman doubles on the horn, collects hounds inside the covert, and blows 'gone away' as hounds stream away out of the covert, on the line of the fox. It is one of the most thrilling moments of the chase. If you do not warm to it, if you do not feel a tingle in your spine, then perhaps you had better stick to some other form of equestrian activity; perhaps indoor dressage. . . .

Your horse will have shared your excitement, and he will certainly want to follow hounds at top speed immediately. If he has absolutely no interest at such times then he is not a hunter, and probably never will be one. You will have to wait until the Field Master signals assent before you start your hunt. It is vital to allow hounds to settle properly on the line at this critical stage, and the first class Field Master is the man who can give the pack and the huntsman every chance to hunt the fox effectively, whilst allowing the mounted field the maximum opportunity to ride the country available.

I will also assume you are fortunate enough to be in a nice piece of grass country with a reasonable variety of hedges and timber fences. This is a big assumption, because it is, alas, the exception rather than the rule in modern Britain, but I will be analysing later the various types of country to be ridden.

More people get into trouble in jumping the first fence in crowded mounted fields than at any stage in a hunt. I have seen even first class horses ridden by Field Masters put in a totally unexpected stop at this juncture. Concentrate hard on giving your horse every chance to see the fence and to take it at the right pace and at the correct angle. Other people may be swerving about, but make sure *your* horse is taken at the obstacle dead straight with ample opportunity to observe it properly. Many horses hit the first fence, or even fall, simply because they are taken at it right on the heels of the horses in front, and they do not know the problem until it is too late.

Queueing at jumpable places is all too often inevitable in the modern hunting field. Some people will crowd closer and closer to the fence as their turn approaches and the opportunity for the horse to jump properly becomes quickly more limited. Even if you do know the country well, do not assume that only one place, or two or three places, in a hedge are jumpable. Use your own initiative whenever possible in developing an eye for the practicable place which no one else is jumping; get there quickly and if your eye and experience tell you all is well, then have a go.

For the real novice I would temper this advice with some cautionary notes. Rather than trying to take your own line willy-nilly, look out for the odd individual who is not following the sheep queueing at a 'safe' place. Do not ride on the heels of the thruster, but if he finds a practicable place and jumps safely further up the fence, then make sure you follow him smartly. Obviously if he has a crashing fall then it is probably a bad place, perhaps with hidden wire on the landing side, but far more often than not the individual who goes on his own will clear the fence more safely and economically than the crowd. He will probably have chosen a more solid-looking place which makes his horse treat it with respect; he will have attacked the fence with impulsion and resolution, and he will have had no risk of interference from the crowd, which is the bane of jumping in queues. Hauling your horse to a halt behind a refuser, or being crashed into by another horse running down a fence as you take off, are some of the least amusing aspects of the hunting field.

'I *do* wish you wouldn't do that,' I exclaimed in disgust recently as a gentleman in Leicestershire shuddered to a halt just in front of me yet again.

He turned in the saddle and agreed dolefully: 'So do I . . . .'

Over-riding is still one of the most dangerous practices in the hunting field, and it is seen far too often. You must not jump immediately behind someone; if he falls, your horse will have very little chance to avoid the fallen horse or rider. If your horse lands on the latter there can so easily be a serious, or even fatal, accident, and it will be your fault.

If you are jumping a fence simultaneously in a crowd then either ride to the right or left of the person in front, or let them land safely before jumping in their tracks. The hunting field should certainly be possessed by a sense of urgency, but it is not a race; no one is getting a prize for being first past the post. You are endeavouring to be with hounds, but you must do this within the bounds of courtesy and consideration for others. The latter particularly applies where riderless horses are concerned. If it is possible then you should certainly catch someone else's horse and return it to him. It may be your turn all too soon.

In Ireland I was secretly congratulating myself on being reasonably well up at the sharp end, for once, in a very good hunt across banks when a lady fell very near me, and with an inward groan I realised that I should have to catch her horse, which would certainly mean losing my hard-won place. I pulled over to catch the creature, but it veered sharply away and galloped through a gateway on to a lane, while hounds continued right-handed. I pursued the riderless horse along the lane for quite a way when suddenly it halted and stood quietly, as hounds appeared like magic from our right, pouring across

One of Ireland's most famous horsemen, Mr P. P.
(Pat) Hogan clearing a ditch off a bank in the
Limerick country. A good man to follow, but a bad
one to beat.

the lane. A group of riders soon jumped the bank down into the lane, and a man approached me with a broad smile and said: 'Thank you for catching my wife's horse; I'll take it to her. You go on . . .'. I turned left and followed the other leading riders over another bank; it gave me a marvellous short cut into the best phase of the run which only a few enjoyed. Virtue is rarely rewarded so promptly in this wicked world.

The art of staying near the front is not simply a matter of galloping flat out. The man whose horse lasts longest has mastered the art of an apparently effortless strong canter which his horse can keep up for many miles. This rider is looking for the next practicable fence as soon as he has cleared one, and he rarely jumps into a field which does not have a possible exit. He keeps an eye on the Field Master whenever possible so that he does not go on to forbidden land, or he takes his own precautions not to commit the crimes of riding on seeds, or stampeding farm stock. If he opens a gate he shuts it, or makes sure the following riders hear his warning shout of 'Gate please!' Above all he watches hounds, pulls his horse up when the pack checks, changes his direction in plenty of time when hounds swing and keeps near them, without riding on their sterns, or getting in front of them on the flanks so that he is in danger of being on the line should they swing. It sounds a formidable task; it is indeed, and this is why one so seldom sees people riding to hounds really beautifully. To do so they need a rare combination of nerve and experience, and a good knowledge of venery and agriculture.

However, there is a great deal of fun in at least striving to emulate these ideals, and it is so much better to try than to be a crashing, bashing sheep in a woolly flock of riders simply playing follow my leader.

When hounds do check, and there is seldom a run without a pause of some sort, keep your eyes firmly on the pack. Resist the temptation to sit back and chat away. If hounds have checked in a wood or some other thick covert it is amazing how they can get away again with few people noticing. You must still give hounds plenty of opportunity to get on the line again unhindered of course, but you will save precious minutes if you are watching closely and are ready to take your place at or near the front of the field.

Always remember that nerve will usually get you over a stiff fence, but it is an eye for the country which will ensure that you complete a run among the leaders. You must endeavour to train your eye. Watch how the hounds jump an obstacle ahead, and observe the rider in front. It is extremely useful to be able to spot in plenty of time that the next fence has a drop to it. It is amazing how many people are taken by surprise by drop fences. If the rider in front partly disappears on landing then he is obviously at a lower level.

It is important in jumping all fly fences to approach them at ninety degrees. Even the most innocent-looking hedge may have a deep, wide ditch lurking on the far side, and the width may vary along the length of the fence. The man on your left may have an easy jump whereas you may be tackling a much wider place. Nowadays there are far too many places in hunting countries where wire oxer fences may also be lurking on the landing side. As I know only too well, a horse catching a foreleg on such wire can be brought down hard, as if in a snare. A hind leg dropped on the wire is slightly less likely to cause a fall, but it can certainly produce horrible gashes and grazes on a horse's stifle. If there is only one practicable place in a fence then you must queue, and should your horse refuse then you must go to the back of the queue, not keep on trying again in front of other people.

Another 'crime' of the hunting field is committed by the horse which dives from an angle at the one practicable place which someone else is already approaching. This is often due to the rider of the offending horse simply not being in control. It can cause nasty falls and collisons; and results all too easily from a horse refusing then running down a fence into the path of other horses jumping. Riding safely in company is an art in itself and the good hunter must be well schooled enough to perform all the manoeuvres necessary to avoid collisions.

Timber may be jumped far more slowly than fly fences. Again, an eye for the country is important. It is no good trotting slowly up to a piece of timber and hopping it if there is a large ditch or scoop on the landing side. Experience and concentration should enable you to look out for such things automatically and to adjust your pace accordingly.

The stiffer and more solid the timber, then the more collectedly you need to jump it. The ability to see a stride is essential in tackling such obstacles frequently. Fortunately, the timber in most countries is fairly simple: straightforward rails which will break if hit hard, or hunt jumps in the form of 'tiger traps', those triangular-shaped frames of timber put into gaps, and first invented, I believe, by the late Arthur Dalgety when he was Master of the Southdown.

I believe the modern hunter should be schooled at home to jump barbed wire safely. You can use string and silver paper as a training obstacle to start with, and progress to lungeing your horse over the real thing (this is not something I would advise the novice to tackle on his own). Capt Ian Farquhar, who is Joint Master and huntsman of the Bicester and Warden Hill country in Buckinghamshire and Oxfordshire, is one of the best exponents I know of wire jumping. He will turn his horse at sheer wire and pop over confidently whenever necessary, saving enormous distances in detours which would otherwise have to be made to stay with hounds.

Nevertheless, barbed wire is awful stuff and I hate it. If you only have one precious horse then I would treat wire with considerable respect, and do not attempt to train him to jump it whilst actually in the hunting field. Such lessons are much better learnt at home.

Again, a practised eye for the country will tell you whether the wire against or near the top of a fly fence can safely be negotiated. One of the most fearsome wired countries I have seen is that of the County Down Staghounds in Northern Ireland; a rolling country, virtually all grass, with many thin, straggly hedges threaded with wire. Your horse must resist the temptation to jump through the hedge instead clearing it as if it were completely solid in order to miss the wre. They have enormously long hunts, with points as much as 19 to 24 kilometres (12 to 15 miles), and the local horses jump the wire constantly with amazing aplomb. These horses also have to cope with every other type of obstacle, and a good, sound animal which has gone well with the County Down should be able to cross any country in England with ease.

The most frequently encountered obstacle in the south of Ireland is, of course, the bank. The chief thing about banks is to give the horse plenty of freedom to use his forehand. Hanging on to your horse's mouth to keep yourself in the saddle is a sure recipe for disaster.

When I first went to Ireland many years ago I was jocularly advised to 'sit forward going up, and lean back coming down'. The second part of this is bad advice. Of course you should lean forward going up the bank, but you should keep forward with your horse coming down also, to ensure that your weight is off his back and loins as he lands. An exaggerated forward seat will do you no good, but certainly keep your weight over the centre of gravity, which means over the shoulders.

For this reason it is advisable always to ride bank countries with a neck strap, and unashamedly to hold on to this whenever necessary, rather than drag on the reins. The technique is to approach a bank at a trot, or even a walk, jump up on to the bank and leap down to the other side. A horse which tries to fly his banks will soon be in trouble.

There is always a ditch on at least one side of the bank, where the earth was dug up to raise the bank. Sometimes banks are faced with stones or slates, and all too frequently there is a strand of wire on the landing or take-off side, or even, horror of horrors, on top of the bank. A great deal of my past life flashed before my eyes as a four-year-old posed on a high bank in the Black and Tan country, delicately picked his feet over a strand of new wire and then launched out over a veritable chasm on the landing side. If he had caught his knees in the wire this book would never have been written.

The large banks, such as you will find in Limerick, Tipperary and many other areas, often have considerable growth on top. This has increased in the postwar years. A horse has to force his way through, and the use of the neck strap is even more important to keep your seat when the briars pull at you. In my experience the big double banks are often easier to jump than the smaller 'single' banks which are narrow-topped and give no room for a horse to actually land. The good Irish hunter will cross these at some speed if necessary, but he will 'lay a leg' on top of the bank as he crosses it, so that he has sufficient purchase to heave over a biggish ditch on the landing side. In England banks are encountered mainly in Cornwall, and these are tackled much the same way as in Ireland.

The next most common type of obstacle in Ireland is the wall, and it is also to be found in parts of England: the Cotswolds has dry limestone walls; Derbyshire offers formidable black stone walls, and limestone is found again in Yorkshire and the Pennines. Walls provide a clean obstacle with a good ground line and horses usually jump them well.

In Ireland some walls are so large they must be banked. I was amazed in Co. Kilkenny by the ease with which an Irish hunter can land on a wall of flinty stones and leap off without much risk of cuts.

The most enjoyable wall country is surely the Galway Blazers' beautiful stretch of light grassland and small walls, where your horse is constantly jumping from one field to the next. In many fields there are no gates; shepherds simply remove the stones to allow the sheep access, and then rebuild the gap. These walls can often be jumped at a strong canter, and it is indeed a delight to follow hounds across the old turf, taking the walls as they come. A young horse which has learnt to jump in this country will usually go on and do well in a fly fence country, provided he is introduced young enough to the mysteries of ditches on the landing sides of English hedges!

Open water is a hazard you may meet in many countries. The old hunting prints of the eighteenth and nineteenth centuries frequently depict mounted followers leaping brooks at a gallop. In Leicestershire, the Whissendine brook is associated with Nimrod's account of a group of riders leaping it at a spot where it was 6 metres (20 ft) wide. 'Who is that under his horse in the brook?' asks one member of the field.

'He will be drowned,' says another.

'I shouldn't wonder,' observes a third.

Nimrod adds the much quoted phrase: 'But the pace is too good to enquire.'

Since the Olympic width for open water in show jumping is 5.48 metres (18 ft) it is of course perfectly justifiable to gallop at a brook 6 metres (20 ft) wide. This is an exceptional jump, of course, but in my experience it is often better *not* to gallop at open water in natural country. A horse can jump an amazing width virtually from a standstill provided he leaps with resolution. I have seen this demonstrated dramatically during fox-hunting with the Meath hounds in Ireland, and with the Ward Union staghounds who run over the same country of fearsome open ditches. The Irish method is usually to walk up to the lip, give the horse his head, and he will do the rest. Sometimes, when the ditch is too wide for a single leap, the Irish hunter will leap on to the slope of the opposite side of the ditch and then scramble up. Even Irish horses get it wrong sometimes; I have jumped these ditches with a man actually riding along at the bottom seeking a way out after a fall!

In East Anglia there are virtually no hedges, and little timber to jump, but the open dykes or ditches are cleared by hunters, and they usually adopt the standing jump method with success. Rather as in jumping off a bank, the rider should take care to give the horse plenty of freedom in the use of his head and neck.

When you are jumping open water, do endeavour to find a firm part of the bank. Old hunting lore says that anywhere near a willow tree on the bank is the safest, but I doubt that you

'Give me the horse that n'eer turns his head . . .'
Mr John Hayes and his hunter not stopping to
open a gate during a day in the South Notts
country.

would have time to look for one. Resolution is a key factor in jumping water successfully; your hunter must feel nothing but confidence down the reins, and through the rider's legs and heels.

It is amazing what courage will accompish. Two seasons ago I was out with the County Limerick foxhounds when we came to the fast-flowing River Deely. Without hesitation the huntsman Hugh Robards and that great horseman P. P. (Pat) Hogan leapt down off the bank, a drop of some 1.20 metres (4 ft) into the river. I saw Pat's horse submerged completely for a few seconds, with Pat up to his chest in water. Then the horse bobbed up and began to swim strongly, the current still carrying it sideways down the wide river. Further down, Pat and Hugh made the opposite bank at a cattle watering place and their horses scrambled out. The rest of the field – including myself – shamelessly rode along the bank to a bridge. Apart from their courage, I marvelled at the hardiness of the two swimmers who hunted on all day wet through in January.

In Britain, I rate the Berkeley country in Gloucestershire as one of the most formidable. Its hunting country between Berkeley Castle and the banks of the Severn is flat, marshy land, drained by reens, which are open, water-filled ditches. The sides are usually cut deep and straight; if a horse gets in he often has a floundering, frightening time getting out. There are often thorn hedges, usually not of a great height, guarding these yawning ditches on the take-off or landing side. You need a bold horse to jump these successfully, but once they are used to the country good hunters perform well.

But the most dangerous places in the modern hunting field are probably gateways and roads. Falls on slippery roads are usually so much worse than elsewhere, because you land on a hard surface, and if you trot or canter on roadside verges you must keep a sharp look-out for the narrow drainage channels which all too easily bring a horse down too.

Beware of slipping up on bad or smooth going. If you are going to jump a gate beware of one which is not properly latched. Hitting a swinging gate will give a horse the worst fall imaginable. I have done it once and just got away with it; I have seen others do it and sometimes have crashing falls.

Do get off your horse and slacken his girths if he has been working hard, perhaps slogging through deep going, and you then have a check at the end of a run. If he is blowing hard and falling behind when the mounted field is galloping then it is probably your fault because he is not fit enough for the job, or you have used him unsparingly and he has simply had enough. Either way, resist the temptation to kick him on; nurse him instead, by pulling him up to a trot or a walk, and take him home as soon as possible if he is really fading.

An alternative problem may be that your horse is wrong in the wind, or going wrong in the wind. If he continues to roar or whistle, have his wind checked by your vet; it may be a case for the Hobday operation (described in more detail in Chapter 3).

One last piece of advice: have fun in partnership with your horse and if on the whole he serves you well, then 'be to his faults a little blind, be to his virtues ever kind.'

CHAPTER 7

Hunter Showing

JUDGING BY the national press, on the comparatively rare occasions that horse shows are mentioned at all in most newspapers, you would imagine that the heart of any show is the main jumping class. In fact, the showing classes are the heart of the matter, and it may be safely asserted that of all the various showing classes, those for hunters are the most important.

Although a type and not a breed, the hunter represents the British riding horse at its best. Newcomers to the horse show scene may be inclined to find the showing classes dull. This is because they do not know what is going on, nor are they aware of the subtleties which may attend the decision-making process. To get the full flavour of judging you need to know the personalties involved, their past and current form with the horses they are showing, and above all the background and foibles of the judges, though the drawback of getting too far 'in' is that the chit-chat at the ringside, the interplay of personalities and the rivalries become an end in themselves. Feuds and rows can all too easily attend any form of showing; the pain of seeing your cherished animal apparently slighted by those omnipotent judges is too much for some people, and all sorts of dramas can result. Compared with many other forms of showing, the hunter classes are not too bad in this respect. The occasional upset is inevitable, but one of the great redeeming features of the game is the benevolent but firm rule of the Hunters' Improvement Society, and the fact that there is a hard core of professional showing men and women who, in the main, have long ago learned the necessity of taking defeat philosophically. The judge is 'king' on his day, but you can test his opinion with another judge elsewhere. If your horse fails regularly then you

Mrs Vin Toulson, wife of one of the most successful postwar show hunter producers, riding the champion hunter, Buckingham – appropriately at Bucks County Show.

might as well accept the inevitable, and find another animal if you want to win.

Although there may appear at first to be an impenetrable mystique about hunter classes, it is not so difficult to get the hang of the thing. Anyone really interested in horses will quickly learn to enjoy this section of a show. Learning how to succeed as a judge or a competitor is another matter, but with the aid of a leading exhibitor of show hunters I will try to throw at least a little light on this mystery in the next chapter.

Crucial to all forms of showing is a unanimity of view as to what type is being sought and inevitably there are confusions and differences of opinion in sorting out the best hunter because of its role as a type rather than a breed. It is not possible to learn how to be a judge from a book, and I have no intention of trying to expound on the best ways to arrive at decisions in the show ring. Common sense is essential, of course, but it must be informed by a deep knowledge of the subject. Above all, the judge must always have in his mind's eye the type that he is looking for, and he must be able to match up the horses in the ring to that type as quickly and accurately as possible.

You will see this art practised to a remarkable degree by the great foxhound judges. Hounds are judged uncoupled at puppy shows and it is wonderful to see a top class judge sort them out swiftly and accurately, sending the least favoured out of the ring until a selection of leading hounds remains to be put in the final placings.

Judging the ridden hunter classes calls for above average horsemanship. Riding someone else's horse for the first time is always daunting, but especially so in the centre of a large ring, before an audience. Judging the novice class at the Royal Dublin Horse Show, for example, calls for quite a lot of nerve as well as skill. It has been known for some exhibitors from way out in the Emerald Isle to interpret 'novice' extremely literally, and animals have arrived in the novice class with little knowledge of a saddle and bridle, let alone the niceties of the show ring.

Judging brood mares and young stock shown in-hand is particularly difficult. Horses can change so much in develop-

Mr 'Tub' Ivens from the Grafton country, riding champion heavyweight hunter Bally Manor at the Royal Highland Show.

ment that it is extremely difficult to make acceptable decisions about a foal or a yearling with an accurate assessment of its potential. Years of experience help, and the man who has had to 'put his money where his mouth is', by buying young stock to sell on later is likely to have his judgement sharpened by the hard school of inexorable profit or loss.

The Hunters' Improvement Society listed forty-two shows in Britain as qualifiers for the Horse of the Year Show in early October when the Hunter of the Year is chosen. These qualifying shows range from the great county agricultural shows to smaller one- or two-day horse shows. The atmosphere in the ring and around it during the hunter classes is unique.

At the start of the season everyone is looking for the new horses brought out by the leading show hunters and riders. A pattern usually sorts itself out during the season, and interest sharpens as judges chop and change the order of the leading

One of the most popular and successful of postwar show hunter producers, Mr Jack Gittins, riding Mr Nat Galway Greer's Marble Arch at Dublin Horse Show. He died in the saddle at Dublin Show in 1977.

horses in the championships at the major shows. Newark and Notts is traditionally the start of the show hunter season in May. The weather may be cold still, and some showing men will delay bringing out their young hopefuls, but this is always an important show, and is full of interest.

The Royal Windsor later in May is the largest outdoor horse show surviving in Britain, now lasting five days, and having a beautiful setting below the walls of Windsor Castle. The patronage of the Queen and the Duke of Edinburgh, who usually drives in the combined driving championship at the show, give this show its unique prestige. Nevertheless, the Royal Windsor is sometimes afflicted by inclement weather and hunter stock from the North is not usually well represented here, but winning at the Royal Windsor is a good start to anyone's season and leading horses are much in evidence.

Because of Northern Ireland's political problems, the Royal Ulster Show later in May probably does not get the attention it deserves elsewhere in the United Kingdom. Ulster is still a splendid breeding area for top quality hunters, and fortunately the political situation does not prevent them going down to Dublin later in the season, sometimes to win the championships from their rivals in the south.

In June the Royal Bath and West and Royal Cornwall are a particular delight because the West Country is a great breeding ground for hunters, and the young stock classes at these shows are well worth seeing. There are also good quality hunter classes at the South of England Show at Ardingly. Mr Douglas Bunn has extended the range of his shows at Hickstead well beyond show jumping, and his spring show is a qualifier for Wembley's hunter classes.

The Three Counties and the Royal Norfolk are the highspots in June. Amazingly, at the time of writing the Royal Highland Show continues not to bother to be a qualifier in the H.I.S. list.

July is traditionally the month when hunter showing in England reaches its peak, with the Royal at the beginning of the month being the setting for the H.I.S.'s own ridden hunter classes, the championship for the Horse and Hound Cup being held on the Monday afternoon. The big ring at Stoneleigh, Warwickshire, the Royal Agricultural Society's perma-

One of the most elegant and successful ladies of the show ring, Lady Violet Vernon, here riding Mr Marshall Parkhill's Monarch to win the Ladies' Lightweight Hunter Class at Dublin.

nent showground, certainly gives a horse room to gallop properly. There have been complaints about the cinder track, but these have been sorted out, and the Royal maintains its position as a great gathering of hunters and hunter enthusiasts.

The Great Yorkshire in July is particularly interesting, not only because of its hunter classes, but because it provides a good opportunity to see Cleveland Bay classes at their best.

The East of England Show is a special focus for hunting people since it also encompasses Peterborough Royal Foxhound Show, and provides a wonderful opportunity to enjoy both horse and hound. It always surprises me that the East of England and the Royal International Horse Show in London continue to clash each year. The latter is now an indoor show held at the Empire Pool, Wembley, a fact which causes many a nostalgic sigh from those of us who so much enjoyed the great days when it was an outdoor show in the spacious setting of the White City arena where there was so much more room in the main ring for hunters and the other showing classes. Now they are judged for conformation and ride in the outdoor rings at

Wembley, and at last enter the main ring for a comparatively brief appearance when they are judged for 'presence' and given final placings.

The supporters of the Royal International taking place indoors point to the fact that it is a guaranteed financial success in this setting no matter what the weather, and the British Horse Society benefits considerably from the profits. True, but on a hot July day one can be forgiven for joining the nostalgic sigh brigade! The Royal Welsh Show also takes place in July and has a good range of hunter classes.

In August the place to be is the Royal Dublin, which I consider the greatest horse show in the world. The setting at Ballsbridge is magnificent, with ample grass rings for the in-hand classes as well as all the ridden ones. The hunters are a feast for the connoisseur, and the hunter championship in the main ring is a major equestrian occasion indeed.

The show is also, of course, a great opportunity to see the Irish Draught horse at its best, and the Connemara pony classes are a treat. The show jumping is splendid because the Irish really dress up such occasions as the Nations Cup with lavish bands and parades; the stewards appear in full morning dress, and there is tremendous excitement accompanying the contests which you will never see matched anywhere else. Above all, the Dublin Horse Show is a great sale of horses. Virtually everything on show is for sale, and you may see prospective buyers looking at the young hunters in the yards at Ballsbridge. Young lads will put their horses, with immense enthusiasm, over battered practice jumps, and shouting Irishmen wave sticks as they lunge young stock over similar obstacles.

Alas, the cream of these horses is usually no longer destined for the English hunting field. The buying is often dominated by gentlemen from Italy, America, or even as far away as South Africa. They are looking for a horse 'with a jump in it', and they mean an exceptional jump. For they are spending big money on show jumpers, hopefully of international class, and I have seen superb horses of hunter type standing in stalls and loose boxes in Italian stables near Milan, condemned never to gallop across country in the wake of hounds, as they were bred to do.

One of the growth areas of hunter showing is the working hunter class. Mrs Robert Oliver rides Major Gittins to victory at Royal Windsor Show.

You may condemn my regret as sentimental, but it is not, for the continued emphasis on high prices for show jumping will not, in the end, do much good to the hunter. The qualities of galloping and immense stamina are not required in show jumping, and it will be a pity if the need to find a horse with a big jump in it overcomes all other considerations in breeding and producing young horses.

After the heady delights of the Royal Dublin there are some good two-day shows in England which qualify for Wembley, ending with a splendid one-day show, the Bucks County at Aylesbury, early in September. It has a friendly atmosphere and I hope it is content to remain a one-day fixture because it is a comfortable size.

The Horse of the Year Show, at the Empire Pool, Wembley, early in October, sets the seal on the success of a show hunter during the season. It is a marvellous show; no one minds being indoors at this end of the year, and the atmosphere is tremendous during the final placings of the hunter classes. It is a great thrill to see one of the great showing exponents, such as David Tatlow, Robert Oliver or Vin Toulson, as they canter round the Wembley ring after a championship presentation. The crowd roars and claps as the spotlight picks out the winning horse; there is a final salute to the royal box, and the rider leaves the ring at a strong gallop.

Mr Bob Dean of British Equestrian Promotions performed a service for hunter showing when he introduced Waterford Crystal as sponsors in Britain. They provide augmented prize money for leading qualifying classes during the season, and for the Show Hunter of the Year award at Wembley. I hope that more can be achieved in the way of sponsorship for hunter showing in general.

Hunters in the United Kingdom and Ireland are judged in classes according to the weight which it is considered an animal is capable of carrying. This may be a matter of considerable contention, and if the judges consider *on the day* that a horse should be in a lower or higher weight category they will arbitrarily transfer it to another class. Objections may be lodged to this, and the matter then has to go to arbitration by H.I.S. officials. Ridden hunters must be a minimum of four years old.

HEAVYWEIGHTS

Heavyweight hunters must be capable of carrying over 88.9 kilos (14 stones). The true heavyweight is particularly difficult to find nowadays because economics are all against producing such animals. It must be understood that show animals emerge from a great reservoir of working animals, and the hunter capable of carrying 97 kilos (15 stone) or more at speed across country is indeed to be prized. He will have quality as well as substance, and this is the most difficult combination to achieve in breeding. A first cross between a Thoroughbred and a heavy mare of cold-blood breeding will all too often simply produce a large, common horse. Heavy horse blood needs to be in the breeding, but probably several generations back.

Among the great heavyweights since the war has been

Mrs Georgina Andrews and her winning ladies' hunter, Amberwin.

Mighty Fine, a liver chestnut gelding by Al Quaim out of a mare by Duke of Sparta, bred in Co. Cork by Mr Patrick Ball and foaled in 1941. Nat Galway-Greer bought him and won the supreme championship in Dublin, and he was then bought by the late Mr Reg Hindley. In 1949 Mighty Fine won nine championships and was Show Hunter of the Year at the first Horse of the Year Show at Harringay.

Mighty Atom, another liver chestnut from Ireland, was also taken to Dublin by Mr Galway-Greer and won the championship in 1948. He was later bought by Mr W. H. Cooper, and went on to win strings of awards in England, including the Hunter of the Year title at the Horse of the Year Show twice.

The 1960s saw something of a dearth of really exceptional heavyweights. Count Robert Orssich expressed it this way in the 1963 *Horseman's Year*:

This year the 'heavies' were disappointing, but of course this type of horse is the hardest of all to find, especially those with real quality and riding action. There are plenty of 'giant cobs' to be found, but where to look for the real galloping 16-stone hunter such as Mighty Fine, Mighty Atom and the great galloping horses of the past?

Certainly in England many more of the championships began to be dominated by lightweights and middleweights from them on. It seems hardly a coincidence that in Ireland in the 1950s there had been a great decline in heavyweight mares on the farms as mechanisation came in apace, and the farmers

One of the great heavyweight hunters of the postwar period, Mighty Atom, owned by Mr W. H. Cooper, and ridden by Mr R. Lester to win the championship at Richmond Royal Horse Show in 1953.

were simply not keeping the old mares from which the quality giants of the past had so often been produced by Thoroughbred sires.

However, in 1973 a striking heavyweight hunter champion emerged from what must be described as an unlikely source, despite the links between the hunter and the racecourse. The skill and deep experience of Mr Vin Toulson was the extra advantage possessed by Prince's Street, a Thoroughbred race-horse by Black Tarquin, a good sire of 'chasers, and out of Flipper, by another successful 'chasing stallion, Flamenco.

Prince's Street finished fourth in a race at Huntingdon in March, 1973, and was bought by Vin Toulson soon after. In June of that year he won the novice hunter class at the South of England show and never looked back, going on to win every-where he was taken. It was most impressive to see him in the ring at the Royal, for a real weight-carrying Thoroughbred with tremendous quality and presence is now so rarely seen. Vin Toulson had done a marvellous job in ensuring the transition from racing fitness to peak show hunter condition, a consider-able feat of horsemastership.

At the Royal Prince's Street 'went through the card'. He won the novice class, the open heavyweights, and the championship for the Horse and Hound Cup. He went on to gain successes elsewhere, missed the Royal International to have a rest, and finally completed a remarkable season by winning the Show Hunter of the Year Award at Wembley. During the season Mr Toulson sold the horse to an insurance company, but retained him to show in the ring. Unfortunately, Prince's Street had been hobdayed in the past and his future as a show horse was ended by the ban imposed by the H.I.S. which I referred to earlier.

MIDDLEWEIGHTS

The show middleweight hunter should be capable of carrying between 79.4 and 88.9 kilos ($12\frac{1}{2}$ and 14 stone). Commercially, this is a weight which has always been in demand in the hunting field. It is somewhat easier to breed and find a middleweight horse with quality than a heavyweight.

The good middleweight show hunter would, in the right hands, probably acquit itself well in horse trials or even in show jumping. It has the conformation and size to stay and the good movement to perform in a balanced manner on all terrains. In the show ring the quality middleweight frequently beats an indifferent heavyweight in the championship, but a judge's eyes are inclined to light up if he happens to see a heavyweight with the quality to match the middleweight. In such cases the heavyweight usually has the championship.

Middleweights can have problems in a show where the hunter classes are divided into only two weights, as this is done at 85 kilos (13½ stone). The good middleweight is up to a bit more than this, and may be sent by the judge up to the 'heavyweight' section, where he then tends to be on the light side compared with most of the others. There were some splendid middleweights just after the war; such horses as Beau Geste, Blarney Stone and Unique were among the winners.

Again, I would quote Count Orssich at the start of the 1960s. This time he is enthusing:

The middleweight section this year (1962) predominated both in quality and quantity, proved by the number of entries at most of the shows, and the fact that more champions were forthcoming from the middleweight classes than from any other denominations.

Here we find such good stamp as Mrs Dean's Viking, Mr H. Haldin's Marksman, Mrs 'Babe' Moseley's Highland Fling, and that really quality middleweight, Mr Hugh Sumner's Tartan Bird.

I consider that middleweights are the most valuable animals, for not only are they capable of doing two-jobs in the show world, viz. their own and the ladies' classes – but they may well be good enough to win 'chases, or at least point-to-points, or combined training thereafter.

In the 1960s at the Royal the championship was captured by Mr Tomkinson's heavyweight Middleton in 1962, and by Mrs Beckwith-Smith's excellent heavyweight Robin Hood in 1963 and 1964. It is significant that from 1965 until Prince's Street's triumph in 1973 the Royal championship invariably went to middleweight horses.

Mrs Waring's Sporting Rights, ridden by Donald Owen, won the championship in 1968, but for the next four years the championship was well and truly captured by Mr Norman Crow and his brilliant middleweights Top Notch and Fair Gin. Mr Crow is the former Master of the North Shropshire Hunt, and farms near Wellington. He is a highly successful breeder as well as an exhibitor in the show ring, in which capacity he won the Prince of Wales Cup for the champion young horse on no fewer than eight occasions at the H.I.S. summer show.

Fair Gin was by Quality Fair, belonging to Mr Charlie Mumford, of the famous Tea Caddy Stud in Northampton-shire. Quality Fair was one of the most influential premium stallions of the last decade.

The success of Fair Gin at the Royal in 1971 and '72 was followed by two years of championship victories by Top Notch, son of another premium stallion, Top Walk. Top Notch also won the Hunter of the Year title at Wembley in 1969 and '70. He had tremendous presence and is remembered as one of the outstanding middleweights of the postwar period.

I had the pleasure of hunting with the North Shropshire while Mr Crow was still Master, and a very good day we had. Mr Crow adopted the splendid policy of hunting his former

The judges' decision is final. Two judges at the Hunters' Improvement Society Stallion Show at Newmarket: Capt George Rich (*left*) and Mr John Daniell.

top show horses, and Fair Gin and Top Notch were among those who were superb mounts in the hunting field.

A particularly nice middleweight to capture honours at the Royal in both 1974 and '75 was Seta Pike, home bred in Yorkshire by Mrs Frank Furness, being sired by the H.I.S. premium stallion Kadir Cup.

Dual Gold, by Le Dieu D'Or, and formerly owned by Lady Zinnia Pollock, won the Horse and Hound Cup at the Royal in 1976 after winning the middleweight section, but the Show Hunter of the Year title that year went to a heavyweight, Ballymanor, ridden by the irrepressible 'Tub' Ivens who part-owned the horse with Mr Richard Tetley from Buckinghamshire. Dual Gold used to be shown successfully by Vin Toulson, but, now owned by Mr White, is currently in the yard of Mr Robert Oliver.

LIGHTWEIGHTS

The H.I.S. ruling on lightweights is that they should be capable of carrying up to 79.4 kilos ($12\frac{1}{2}$ stone). I once heard an eminent Master of Foxhounds exclaim in disgust at the ringside at Dublin: 'But a lightweight simply can't win a championship. It's just not a proper hunter. If it cannot carry more than 13 stone across country then it isn't doing the job for which it was supposed to be bred.'

This is something of an extreme view, but it is true that the advent of lightweights as hunter champions is something of a postwar phenomenon and reflects the decrease in competition from the heavyweights. Some will assert that lightweight hunters have improved, far more being produced with 'presence' as well as quality. I doubt, however, whether the current crop of lightweights would really have prevailed in championships over the heavyweight giants of the past.

Just after the war Wavering Bee, owned by Mr W. H. Cooper, was a famous lightweight hunter in England, winning the championship at the White City and the Champion of England Gold Cup at Peterborough. This was indeed a feat in the days when prejudice against lightweight champions was much stronger than it is now.

Miss Patricia Cope's lightweight Mighty Grand was a big winner in the 1950s, capturing the Show Hunter of the Year award at Haringey in 1955 and '56. He was yet another horse from Ireland, found by the perceptive Mr Galway-Greer.

Mr Ronnie Marmont, that great producer of show horses, had a marvellous lightweight called Cufflink who won championships at many shows, including the White City.

Swagger, ridden with great style side-saddle by Lady Violet Vernon, was a great force as a lightweight and won the Hunter of the Year award in 1961.

At the Royal International Horse Show in 1966 the line up for the championship was led by the lightweight Monbra, exhibited jointly by Mrs R. Cook and Miss Profumo, with another good lightweight as reserve, Mr C. R. Tomkinson's Blue Sujan. It was a sign of the times indeed to see two lightweights ousting the other weight classes so decisively in an important championship.

Over the next ten years middleweights tended to hold sway in hunter championships, but in the late 1970s the hunter

With the walls of Windsor Castle as a background, hunters line up in the main ring at Royal Windsor Horse Show, one of the earliest fixtures of the summer season.

showing world had a lightweight champion which underwent a process of radical reassessment. Bunowen, a brown Irish lightweight by Seven Bells, was brilliantly shown by David Tatlow to win the Horse and Hound Cup at the Royal, and the Show Hunter of the Year Award at Wembley in both 1977 and '78. At the start of 1979 there was a surprise at the Notts and Newark Show when, under new ownership, he was ordered by the judges to be up-graded to the middleweight class. At the Royal Windsor he duly appeared as a middleweight and won his class, but in the championship he stood reserve to Robert Oliver on the heavyweight Flashman. Arbitration referees decided later that Bunowen should henceforth show as a middleweight.

SMALL HUNTERS

If the lightweight hunter is an anathema to some diehards then the small hunter class might be expected to cause them even higher blood pressure. Such classes were introduced not long after the war, originally to give young riders a chance to compete in hunter classes without coming up against the crack professionals. It did not work out this way, as no overall age limit was imposed at the shows. Older riders began to take part from the start, and some of the professionals certainly had a hand in producing the horses.

The H.I.S. ruling for this class is different from the others, in that it specifies height and not weight, the limit being 15.2 hands; adding 'half an inch allowed for ordinary shoes', a ruling which betrays the attention to detail which matters so much in showing.

The small hunter's popularity obviously has some connection with its size which means it is easier and more economical to breed and to keep. It must not be a weedy version of a hack, however, but ideally should exhibit plenty of quality with enough substance to inspire the belief that it really will carry someone across country all day. With so many ladies and teenagers hunting nowadays, there is a great demand for this sort of quality riding horse, and they have so many other uses, ranging from horse trials to riding club activities, and, dare one say it for a hunter, dressage.

The Small Show Hunter of the Year title at Wembley in 1978 was won by Mrs Olive Jackson's Misty Day, a 15.1½ h.h. bay gelding by No Argument, out of Coole Colein. Among the most successful small hunters in recent years has been the Countess of Inchcape's Sporting Print, which won the Wembley title twice, in 1974 and again in 1975 for Miss J. Andrew.

LADIES' HUNTER

One of the aesthetic pleasures of the show ring is the revival in side-saddle riding. It is not mandatory in all ladies' hunter classes by any means, but at the Royal, for example, there is a ladies' hunter class to be ridden side-saddle.

The ladies' is not a specific weight class, but is open to hunters 'suitable for, and to be ridden by a lady'. Lightweights tend to predominate, but good middleweights often win these classes. Much depends on the ride, and manners are put at a particularly high premium. The good-looking horse which takes a firm hold and endeavours to 'cart' the lady judge when she rides it will find itself at the end of the line pretty quickly.

Considering the rising costs of everything, it is perhaps surprising that side-saddle riding should have come in again. Much help has been given by the Ladies' Side-saddle Association, whose chairman and co-founder is Mrs Janet Macdonald from Surrey. She and her colleagues give advice on obtaining side-saddles, the correct method of wearing a side-saddle habit, and instruction in side-saddle riding technique. It is particularly important that a show hunter, shown under a side-saddle, should have a good front, for riding this way sets off the shoulder noticeably.

Whilst the show ring can take some plaudits for the revival in side-saddle riding, I give most credit to those elegant and intrepid ladies who have continued to grace the hunting field in this style, despite the great decline in the practice since pre-war times.

In Leicestershire Lady Margaret Fortescue continues the tradition set by her mother in crossing the Quorn country with tremendous dash and flair. Mrs Fred Barker, wife of the Joint

Winning line-up: (*left to right*) Mr Vin Toulson on Dual Gold, Hunter Champion at Bucks County Show with Peter Richmond and Overflow, Reserve, and Mr Tub Ivens with Bally Manor.

Mrs Betty Gingell, Master and huntsman of the Cambridgeshire Harriers, is a leading figure in the showing world. She is riding Badger to win the Hunter Championship at the Lincolnshire Show.

Master of the Quorn, is another who brings particular elegance and style to the hunting field with an immaculate side-saddle ensemble. In the north, Mrs Malcolm Sherwin, whose husband was Joint Master of the Bedale, and her sister, Mrs Holt from the Sinnington country, both ride side-saddle in the hunting field and in team cross-country rides.

The Duke of Beaufort's country still sees a number of side-saddle riders, including Mrs Gerald Darling, and Lady Dill who came from the Limerick country where she crossed the great banks side-saddle with much aplomb.

The person who has always ridden astride regards jumping fences side-saddle with some awe. I must confess that I am always impressed when I see Lady Margaret Fortescue and her grey hunter nonchalantly jumping five-barred gates. I am assured that side-saddle riding is, in fact, safer. While I concede that this may be so my mind began to boggle when I discovered, for a start, that there are no less than four different ways of mounting a side-saddle! However, it *is* good news that more ladies are riding side-saddle in showing classes and in the hunting field.

One valid point about ladies' hunters is that, provided it has the manners, there is absolutely no reason why a lady's horse should not be well above her weight. Indeed, Mrs Ulrica Murray Smith, Joint Master of the Quorn, and one of the most experienced and accomplished riders across country, has always stated a strong preference for the big horse with ample weight in reserve. One reason is that it has the substance to withstand the regular hard work of the hunting field, and another important point is that it is better equipped to stay on its feet if other members of a large mounted field crash into it!

NOVICE HUNTERS

The stipulation for novice classes is that a hunter should not have been awarded a first prize worth £15 before entries close. This is a vital class in the big shows because, of course, it is a great opportunity to see the new show horses being brought into the game. With costs rising, and show hunter prizes remaining extremely modest compared, say, with those for show jumping, it has often been remarked upon with surprise that so many owners stay faithful to hunter showing. There have been dire warnings about dropping standards and lack of entries. In fact, hunter showing has remained remarkably resilient and at the start of the 1979 season there were some very attractive new horses appearing at the early shows.

WORKING HUNTERS

The working hunter class was imported to Britain from the United States and Canada where it was, and still is, exceedingly popular. A need was felt for a hunter showing class which in some way related conformation and movement to some evidence of performance there and then, in front of the judges.

As a chap 'wot hunts' I have always regarded working hunter classes as something of a puzzle. Since my working hunters are hard at work all the winter in the hunting field they are roughed off in the spring and turned out to grass for the summer before coming to work again in the autumn. How could such working hunters take part in shenanigans in the show ring during the summer months?

I was once ill-advised enough to ask such a question about Foxford, the best hunter I have ever had, putting the question to a young lady who knows more about equitation than I shall ever aspire to, and she replied crushingly: 'Oh, he's not a real working hunter type; he doesn't move well enough. So I shouldn't bother to show him; just keep hunting him.'

This does at least illustrate that not only is there a gulf between the show working hunter and the show hunter, but also between the show working hunter and the sort which actually does the work in the hunting field. Nevertheless, it must be admitted that working hunter classes both for horses and ponies have caught on tremendously in the postwar years. Their advantages are that they provide ring experience for young horses who will probably go on to other things, and they

Mr Roy Trigg riding Aristocrat to win the Hunter Championship at the South of England Show.

certainly put a bit of extra value on to a nice sort of horse. Eventing ladies and gentlemen like to take their horses into anything and everything in order to gain experience before the rigours of their spring and autumn horse trials, and they frequently appear in working hunter classes. Certainly these classes provide an outlet for the horse which is not 'showy' enough for the pure show classes, but can perform adequately to impress the judges, and has good conformation and movement.

Where there are two working hunter classes they divide at 85 kilos (13 stones 7 lbs). If shows wish, in order to save time, they can use two judges, one to judge the conformation while the other is judging the ride.

The H.I.S. merely states that 'suitable fences of natural appearance must be available'. They have to be 'not easily dislodged', a minimum of six in number and a maximum of 1.14 metres (3 ft 9 ins) in height. The 'manner of going' has to be taken into account, with refusals being severely penalised.

The riding judge does not actually have to jump the horses himself, but simply to test the animal's paces. I seem to recall Capt Brian Fanshawe, Joint Master and huntsman of the North Cotswold, having a lovely time jumping the working hunters he was judging on the Arena North ground in Lancashire recently. This predominantly show jumping arena is built on several levels, and the director, Chris Coldrey, had gone to a lot of trouble in providing a really attractive working hunter course. Capt Fanshawe – one of the best men across country I have ever seen – was not going to miss the chance of enjoying it too!

The formula for judging working hunters is 40% for jumping and 60% for conformation, movement, manners and presence, as in a normal showing class. The jumping itself is judged 30% for performance and 10% for style. This formula gives considerable discretion to the judges, which is right and proper, and to the course builders. Probably the most interesting working hunter course I know is that built by Mr Douglas Bunn at Hickstead. He believes fervently in hunters really having to perform adequately, and his working hunter course includes a stone wall and some water ditches. The first time the course was used it caused quite a number of competitors to stop in their tracks, and I was amused to note that one working hunter owner had even taken the precaution of having the world show-jumping champion David Broome as his rider!

The Broome family has recently achieved a great deal with working hunters. David's sister Mary won the Working Hunter of the Year Championship at Wembley in 1977 and '78 with Let's Go, a 16.2 h.h. chestnut gelding by Chou Chin Chow. Beautifully produced, and as one would expect from that stable, a splendid performer over fences, Let's Go is indeed a worthy champion.

Working hunter champions in recent years have included such outstanding horses as Portman Lad, produced by that

Mr Vin Toulson with Princes Street, a real weight carrying Thorough-bred who came from the racecourse to win hunter showing championships.

considerable specialist in this class, Mrs Charles Cope, who is now showing Jonjo with much success. Morning Glory, shown by Roy Trigg, Mrs T. C. Queen's Fidelio, and Capt Turwhitt-Drake's Mister Perkins, are other working champions which have caught the eye in recent times.

BREED CLASSES

The breed classes in hunter sections of horse shows are, of course, of crucial importance. The class headings approved by the H.I.S. are: brood mare with own foal at foot; foal – colt, gelding or filly – foaled in the current year; yearling; two-year-old; and three-year-old. The yearling class is open to colts, geldings or fillies, but colts are not included in the two-year-old and three-year-old classes.

The H.I.S. stipulates that hunter breeding classes are open to the produce of any stallion 'and should not be confined to animals sired by Thoroughbreds'. Nevertheless Thorough-bred-sired stock predominates, although whether we shall see a marked change in view of plans to introduce more substance into hunter breeding through Irish Draught and/or Cleveland Bay stallions remains a matter for speculation.

Stallions I have already described the H.I.S. Stallion Show at Newmarket, and the National Hunter Show at Shrewsbury in the summer where over 400 mares and young stock are on show. These were mentioned in Chapter 3 because of their vital links with the H.I.S. premium breeding system. The King George V Challenge Cup for the best stallion in the show at Newmarket has been won seventeen times by one man, the amazing Mr Charlie Mumford of the Tea Caddy Stud, at Hannington, near Northampton. His stallion Bleep won the championship in 1963–65 consecutively, but the most successful, and indeed influential of his stallions has been Quality Fair, champion for four successive years, 1969 to 1972. Quality Fair was born in 1960, sired by Hook Money, out of Fairy Flower, and was retired as a four-year-old after racing on the flat and over hurdles.

Another exhibitor with considerable achievements since the

A grand heavyweight of the good old sort: Robin Hood, owned by Mrs John Beckwith-Smith, and ridden to victory here by Mr Harry Bonner at Richmond Royal Horse Show.

war has been Mr Bill Manning from Buckinghamshire whose Henry Tudor won the King George V Cup in 1948 and '49, while his Border Legend was the winner in 1959 and '60.

A significant winner in 1962 was Mr L. B. Bloomfield's Solon Morn, a stallion of considerable importance as a successful sire of hunter stock. I have much admired Solon Morn's progeny in the show ring and working in the hunting field.

Recent King George V winners include Armagnac Monarch, in 1973, whose owner at the time, Mr George Maundrell, had narrowly missed winning the championship seven times, five of them with the splendid stallion Game Rights who has been a remarkably influential sire.

In 1974 the champion was Arthur Sullivan, by Talgo, out of Donna Lucia, and owned by Mr A. L. 'Boss' Masters from Bodmin, who is renowned throughout the West Country as a

Mr David Tatlow riding Bunowen, a show hunter which was twice Show Hunter of the Year at Wembley, then became the centre of controversy when it was upgraded from lightweight to middleweight classes.

producer of fine stock. Right Flare was the 1975 winner, and in 1976 Mr Charlie Mumford again took the honours with Royal Clipper, by Ballymoss out of Roseian. Royal Clipper also won the District Class 2 from Mr John Rawding's BP. The 1977 winner was Major Sol, by Major Portion, out of Manilla II, bred by Capt F. G. Barker, Joint Master of the Quorn, for Mrs Roberts, whose late husband, Mr Bill Roberts, stood Solon Morn and other leading stallions. The 1978 winner was Mr Jimmy Snell's Saunter, by Charlottesville out of Padella, who was by the Derby winner St Paddy.

Of considerable importance is the result of the Henry Tudor Challenge Cup competition which is awarded to the current stallion with the best marks achieved in the number of mares served the previous season, and the foaling percentages. Quality Fair won this cup in 1975 and previously as long ago as 1967.

Game Warden was the 1977–8 winner, and other influential sires to win it in recent years include Kadir Cup, owned by Mr Max Abram whose stud in the Middleton country in Yorkshire has a splendid list of hunter stallions in recent years including Foxstar and Weathercock.

Brood mares and young stock The most coveted trophy at the H.I.S. National Hunter Show in the summer at Shrewsbury is the Edward Prince of Wales Cup for the champion young horse. Recent winners include Solgar in 1976, shown by Norman Crow. Solgar was a bay three-year-old non-Thoroughbred gelding, by the premium stallion Solon Morn, and out of Cathy Garnette by Little Cloud.

Major Tim Hellyer, a distinguished judge as well as an exhibitor, whose wife is Joint Master of the Cottesmore, won the Walker Okeover Cup that year for the best filly, with his home-bred chestnut three-year-old, Heron, by Commandeer.

Small Hunter of the Year at the 1978 Horse of the Year Show: Misty Day, owned by Mrs Olive Jackson, and ridden by Mr Michael Poole. This is a hunter class difficult to define, but most judges prefer a compact 'butty' sort of horse.

The H.I.S. champion mare was the Thoroughbred Newton More, a bay daughter of Game Rights, owned by Col and Mrs Tony Coote, while the winning lightweight mare was Crown Emerald, belonging to Miss Joanna Varden who performs a great service in the horse world through her national foaling bank at Meretown Stud in Newport, Shropshire, which provides emergency fostering for orphaned foals. This takes considerable planning and devotion to duty, since time is obviously crucial in saving such foals.

In 1977 the Edward Prince of Wales Cup went to a two-year-old, Fair Sport, by Quality Fair out of Pheasant Rights, by Game Rights. Fair Sport was bred by Miss S. Harrison of Walsall in Staffordshire, and is owned by Mr Ian Thomas, the Queen's dressmaker. That year the H.I.S. champion mare was Cathy Garnette, who had won the same award two years earlier. Cathy Garnette is by the premium stallion Little Cloud, by the Derby winner Nimbus out of Little Britain by Epigram, and is owned by Mr Jimmy Snell. The three-year-old Stardust V, by Foxstar out of Tom's Love by Weathercock, won the 1977 Walker-Okeover Cup for the champion filly, and the champion foal was Miss S. A. Morris's Bruntwood Negative, by Colour Photo out of Tara II by Top Star, bred by Miss Morris in Cheshire.

One of the most important features of the National Hunter Show is the class for produce groups, the award going to the relevant stallion. The great Quality Fair emerged triumphant in 1977, gaining yet another award for the Tea Caddy Stud.

The 1978 National Hunter Show was especially fascinating because the Edward Prince of Wales Cup for the champion young horse went to none other than the great star of three-day eventing, Miss Sheila Willcox, sadly no longer able to compete through injuries, but a great producer of dressage and eventing quality stock. She had purchased the non-Thoroughbred Henry James at Doncaster sales and he was beautifully produced by Robert Oliver to win the Prince of Wales Cup and the Lloyds Bank championship for the best horse in the show. Henry James is by Armagnac Monarch out of Stockton Star, by Game Rights. The winning brood mare in 1978 was My Rougette, a Thoroughbred by Langton Heath, owned by Mrs

H. S. Jeffs. My Rougette's dam was Rouge Croix, by Erin's Pride from the West Country.

HUNTER SHOWING IN AMERICA

Hunter classes in American shows are linked to jumping performance and in some respects resemble the working hunter competition in Britain.

Young stock is, of course, shown in hand; ridden hunters are divided into 'green' or 'regular' sections in breeding, conformation or working classes.

Under the rules of the American Horse Shows Association a 'green' hunter is a horse of any age in his first or second year of showing. First year 'green' hunters are required to jump 1.07 metres (3 feet 6 inches); second year 'green' hunters 1.14 metres (3 feet 9 inches).

The 'regular' section hunter class is, in effect, open but is divided into 'A', 'B' and 'C' Sections. Jumping is required in both the 'conformation' and 'working' classes, but performance is more heavily accepted in the latter.

There is 1.22 metres (4 feet) minimum height allowance in 'A' and 'B' and 1.14 metres (3 feet 9 inches) in 'C'.

Both the 'green' and 'regular' sections are further divided into weight sections, small, lightweight, middleweight and heavyweight. There are also separate classes for Thoroughbred and non-Thoroughbred hunters, and a class for a 'Qualified Hunter' which is simply a horse which has been hunted 'regularly and satisfactorily' with a registered pack of hounds.

The American horse showing scene places much emphasis on the turnout of the rider in its 'Corinthian', 'Appointment' and 'Formal Hunting Attire' classes. 'Corinthian' classes are confined to amateurs in hunting dress, and the rules are exceedingly detailed on the required dress.

Hunter judging is scored on soundness, conformation and performance.

Hunter jumping courses simulate obstacles found in the hunting field as much as possible, and include post and rails, brush fences, stone walls, white board fences or gates, chicken coops, hedges and oxers.

CHAPTER 8

Hunter Showing – Some Expert Advice

OBSERVE A ridden hunter showing class carefully, and you will soon learn something about the technique of judging and exhibiting. It is, however, the tip of the iceberg, and there is much which you cannot learn on the showground.

The horses enter the ring, and at a signal from the steward standing near one or two bowler-hatted judges in the centre, the riders ride round the circumference. They are required to trot, walk, canter and gallop. At this stage the judges can pick out the good movers, and indeed they will have formed preliminary judgements on the conformation of the horses as well.

After this first opportunity to show their horses, the exhibitors are 'pulled in' to the centre of the ring by the stewards, at the judges' behest. Considerable discretion is given to the judges, but invariably the horses which have given the most favourable first impression are put to the left-hand end of a line facing them, and if the class is big enough, a second line of less favoured horses stands behind. Each horse is in turn ridden by a judge, being taken round the ring at all paces. It is quite easy, and sometimes amusing, to see which horses are not giving the judges a good ride. Much tail-swishing, some pulling, and horror of horrors, a buck, can be seen to accompany a bad ride. Saddles are taken off, and the judge or judges now begin to look at each animal closely and critically. They run their hands down the horses legs, and each animal, stripped of its saddle, is taken out of the line up and trotted out in front of the judges so that they may test its soundness and straightness of action.

The horses saddled up again and remounted to be sent round the ring for the judges to see them in action once more. This time the 'pulling in' is crucial, as the judges will now endeavour to place the horses in their approximate final order. Even at this stage I have seen judges show some indecision and clearly change their minds, as the riders are asked to change position in the line. Finally the winner is asked to step forward, accompanied by much clapping from the stands and brave smiles from the vanquished. The cloak of authority suddenly drops from the judge, who becomes just another show official as he goes off quietly for a welcome sandwich.

To get a better idea of the challenge and the methods taken by a top producer of show hunters I went to Gloucestershire where I was privileged to inspect the show yard of Robert and Gill Oliver near Newent.

Robert is one of the most successful producers of hunters, hacks and cobs. He works in partnership with Gill who does much of the groundwork at home, and who is most successful in the show ring in her own right, especially with working hunters. Her father is Mr John Blakeway, chairman of the British Show Jumping Association, a former Master of the Croome Hunt, and still a keen rider to hounds, nowadays with the Belvoir.

Robert Oliver lunges a four-year-old: 'everything depends on how you do it . . . we do not go in for gadgets here.'

I was much impressed by the order and method so apparent in Robert Oliver's yard. He has a mouth-watering collection of horses, kept and shown for a number of owners. There was the champion cob, Master Kempley, Tenterk, the champion hack, and Dual Gold, the splendid middleweight hunter. Flashman, the heavyweight hunter, looked well in his comfortable loose box, and well he might, for soon after I saw him he was to win the hunter championship at the Royal Windsor with Robert in the saddle.

There was also a remarkable collection of new and promising horses, hunters and hacks mostly, some with the show ring as their first objective, others being aimed at the hunting field straight away. Robert and Gill hunt enthusiastically with their local hounds, the Ledbury, and also with the nearby Berkeley which has one of the stiffest and most interesting countries in Britain. It includes the reens on the flat land by the River Severn: those open, water-filled ditches which take confident jumping. There are also formidable hedges with wide ditches to be cleared. The Olivers can go 'like smoke' across country and Robert is a great believer in the hunting field as a place to improve and help to make young horses.

Born at Hereford, he picked up a lot of early knowledge from his grandfather, a master farrier. Robert rode the famous Cusop show ponies for Mr and Mrs Vivian Eckley when he was a boy. Later he worked for Col J. R. Cleghorn who kept good quality hunters, and for Mr Derek Crossman who was Master of the South Herefordshire hounds. Robert whipped-in and helped to make young Thoroughbred horses. Since he set up on his own, Robert has earned a great reputation as a producer of hunters and hacks. The latter have included such great names as Lady Teller, Right Royal and Young Apelles.

It is always impressive to see Robert Oliver in the show ring, especially on the big occasion. He has that great ability to communicate his own calmness to his horses. They go for him beautifully, and they stand relaxed in the centre of the ring when he requires them to do so. I have seen him chuck the reins at a quality Thoroughbred hack when standing after an award, and the animal stood quietly and happily without a thought of taking off or otherwise misbehaving.

Opening a gate on the farm: Robert Oliver believes it is an important element in nagging a show horse. His mount here is champion heavyweight Flashman.

Robert Oliver is one of the most modest and yet articulate of men in the showing world, and I was fortunate to be able to interview him on his art and craft, and to distil some of his answers into the following observations on hunter showing:

I think general standards of riding have improved, if anything, and show horses tend to be going better nowadays, and have a better prospect of eventing successfully, or doing well in some other form of equitation.

In the past there may well have been a tendency to over-show too many horses and one never heard of them again once they had given up the ring. They may well have gone hunting eventually, but they were always looked upon as show horses, intended for no other job. Nowadays the great problem is horsemastership. In the past people had a stud groom, or an old family groom, who did a vital job in looking after their horses. But today, through economy as much as anything, more people have to do their own horses. Although they do not mean to be ignorant, unfortunately there *is* a lot of ignorance, coupled with a reluctance to take advice from older people.

I learnt a lot from a great horse-coper in Herefordshire, Ernie Evans, who was wonderful at breaking, making and selling horses. I think the

136

thing that gets forgotten most in showing is attention to detail. This means that you take a lot of time and trouble fitting the tack, and that the horse is in a relaxed frame of mind.

It is essential to have a horse in top condition, going well with good manners, but it must also have freedom of movement, and this is not easy to achieve. If you overwork a horse you get his mind wound up, and the more work you give him the fitter he will be, which is not necessarily what you want in a show horse. I can always remember an old boy telling me that a show horse should be 'fat and quiet' for the ring, and for the judge. There is nothing worse for a judge than getting on a strange horse, and wondering: 'Is he, or isn't he, is he going to pop off; is he going to drop me?'

When you are judging you want to get on a horse in the ring while he just stands there. You tell him to walk, and he pricks his ears and you give him a pat. Then he trots when you want, and he canters when you ask him, and when he goes into his gallop he comes back to you quietly and simply . . . that's what you really want. It is a question of basic manners and horsemanship.

Our secret when we get a young green horse is to hack him about and keep turning him out in the field. You have to keep their minds right; it is the same with people – if their minds aren't settled or relaxed then they cannot achieve very much.

Dual Gold, Mrs Peter White's brilliant middleweight show hunter, one of the stars of Robert Oliver's yard.

I must be quite honest: when it comes to groundwork, basic schooling on the flat, I do very little, but Gilly does quite a lot. I like hacking them about, and I will not have a horse which will not co-operate properly when I open and shut a gate. Unless he will do what I want when I ride him round the farm, I will not continue working him round in circles for endless periods of groundwork. My method is really getting back to the old-fashioned nagsman's way of working, against modern schooling. I think modern schooling is splendid, but I am afraid that so many younger people work horses in too small an area. They put X number of yards of schooling surface down, and work a horse for two hours in a very small area, which is a great pity.

We do all the normal things with young horses – lungeing, long reining, schooling – but everything depends on how you do it. The Abbot Davies balancing rein, draw reins, or a double bridle are only tools of the trade and what matters is the person who is using them. In fact, we do not go in for 'gadgets' here, but I am a stickler for a horse behaving itself at all times.

Our young show horses get out in the hunting field, and our favourite thing is gate-shutting at the back with these novices. It is the finest

Another illustrious resident at the Oliver yard – Swanbourne, the lightweight hunter which won the Royal International Horse Show championship.

education for any horse, and I am afraid that too many horses are hunted 'up the front' before they are ready. People wonder why their horses pull or refuse, but the reason is that they have done too much too soon. That young horse refusing at a fence in the hunting field should never have been put at such an obstacle at a fast pace so early in its life. Ocassionally you have the sort of young horse with the right temperament that you can take to the opening meet and hunt, and the next time you take him out he is all right. But nine times out of ten you will come unstuck doing that. Of course economics come into it; people are short of time, and a lot of them will not put in the time or trouble to go cub-hunting. They suddenly produce horses at the opening meet and then expect them to behave.

The thing I really will not stand is horses kicking out hunting. I have seen horses' legs broken, and the horses having to be shot, and I have seen people's legs broken by kicking horses. People will not catch hold of a horse's head and thrash it as soon as it kicks.

Quite often with a young show horse I will take it to a show just to get it used to its surroundings, without actually going into the ring. At shows where it is really pouring with rain, and cold and windy, if I think a lot of a young horse I will keep him in the box and take him home. He is either not going to enjoy showing, or he is going to get a chill, and perhaps not give the judge a good ride. When one has gone to an awful lot of trouble, why risk forfeiting the horse's whole career just for the sake of one show?

A young horse needs to be taken to a show and just hacked about to see the sights. Alternatively, take him to a hunter trial and do the same. You cannot expect to produce a horse on winning form in the show ring if it has never left home before.

We spend enough time on our horses to ensure that they will all go well in a double bridle in the show ring. In the old days, of course, a double bridle was not looked upon as 'a gadget', or as a severe bridle. There is nothing nicer than a horse going hunting in a double bridle; you can lift him on the snaffle, or lower him on the curb. There is nothing worse than a horse leaning on you, or snatching at you, or pulling you about.

We never bother with gag bits here. These have become necessary for too many horses because they are allowed to gallop on before they are ready. Of course one has to be practical, and time is money, but you cannot get away from the facts.

I do not think a lot of damage results from a standing martingale. It takes a lot of pressure on the horse's nose instead of on the bit. A tight running martingale exerts pressure on the bars of the horse's mouth. I

Robert Oliver and his wife Gill with Swanbourne, Dual Gold and Flashman.

have seen horses ridden most successfully in standing martingales in the Berkeley country; it is standard equipment there because it lowers the horse's head to make him look where he is going, and what he is doing. You cannot interfere with a horse's mouth with a standing martingale. The argument that a horse cannot spread or jump a ditch when wearing a standing martingale is quite ridiculous. You are not allowed to show a horse in a martingale, but I do believe in riding a young horse about with a standing martingale. If a bird flies out of a hedge and startles him his head goes up immediately, but if he has got a martingale set at the angle where his head should be, neither too high nor too low, it will take the pressure on his nose and not on his mouth.

Whenever I ride a novice horse into the ring, I never 'get after him' as such. I have to think of his future. So I like him to walk in on a long rein. I do not believe in giving novice horses a lot of work on the show ground outside the ring: they should have had all that at home.

In his canter in the ring I like a horse to move nicely, but to be going on. Three-quarters of the people in the show ring make the mistake of over-galloping. They try to gallop round the corners, whereas there the horse should have his hocks underneath him, and just lengthen his stride going down the straight past the grandstand. On the following corner you should use your hands and legs to get him back together to be balanced in turning that corner. But so many people, once the steward beckons them to gallop, go away flat out, and this is where so many horses are spoilt. They learn to cut their corners and to anticipate the gallop. This is why you see so many horses throwing their heads, completely unbalanced, and getting ring crafty in their first season. Instead they should be ridden on the outside of the ring and not try to cut corners, nor to dodge about from corner to corner trying to catch the judge's eye. People worry too much about that. If only they would stay on the outside position and use the whole of the ring, going out round the corners, the judge would see them better, and the horse would have a much improved ride. You do not have to get close to the judge for him to see your horse properly.

Robert Oliver is a great believer in long reining; manners are all important and it takes immense patience as well as skill to achieve show hunter standards.

Much of the groundwork on the horses in the Oliver yard is carried out by Gill, seen here schooling lightweight hunter Swanbourne.

What I should like to see, either in the hunter championships or possibly in the weight classes at the bigger shows, is a change of rein. In showing, from the day the horse enters the ring to the day he is finished, nine times out of ten he will be ridden right-handed round the ring. Unfortunately, some judges automatically do this too when they ride the horses. It does no good to horses constantly to ride them in the same direction. This is why, I am afraid, 75% of show horses are 'one-sided'.

I remarked earlier on the old old boy advising me to have my horses 'fat and quiet'. In fact, you will never see me in the ring with a fat show horse. The art in conditioning show horses is to hit the happy medium. They have to be reasonably fit because it is surprising how strenuous a day at a show can be for a horse. He may leave home at 6 a.m. and not get home until 9 p.m. This takes a great deal out of a horse mentally as well as physically, and all too soon he can become tucked up. Basically most show horses should be fitter than they are. We give ours quite a lot of road work at the start of the season to help in this respect.

When I buy a potential show horse I pay a lot of attention to tempera-

Show Hunter of the Year at the Horse of the Year Show, 1979, Mrs P. White's Flashman, at Robert Oliver's yard near Newent, Glos.

ment as well as conformation. I hate to go into a horse's box and see either his hind end swing round, or his ears laid back. I do not think sharp, gassy sorts of horses make the best hunters, eventers, or race-horses, although occasionally you get the exception to this rule. It is very difficult to find show horses nowadays, and when you do find them they are often doing an entirely different sort of job. Too many beautifully topped horses are nowadays being bred without enough bone below the knee. Many people make a great mistake in imagining that a horse has got to be tall to carry a lot of weight. This simply is not so if his conformation is right.

Nearly all my horses have been by H.I.S. premium stallions or locally bred. I am fortunate to live in a part of the world where a lot of good horses are bred by all sorts of people. Flashman is the first Irish-bred show horse I have had.

One problem in the in-hand showing classes is the way these young horses are handled by some people. They not only ruin them for showing but for any other sort of job later on. If they have got a lovely young horse too many people in England tend to over-nanny them because they are afraid of something happening to them. They bring them in at night, and put them out by day, and rush them in again if it starts to rain. It is much better if the horse is either out or in. If he is going to a show next day by all means bring him in the night before, but do not keep him in *all* the time rugged up; this is an artificial way of keeping a young horse which is much better living out most of the time.

Some of the young led horses nowadays are worn out before they even start to mature; you can see this by looking at their limbs, and it is due to continually being dragged about the countryside, travelling from show to show. Unfortunately, as soon as the young horse wins a prize his owners are busy looking through the catalogues to find somewhere else to take him as soon as possible. They are not content to take him once a week. A certain amount of showing is perfectly all right, but it needs to be kept within sensible limits.

The other problem is that young horses become 'one-sided' through being continually led on the near side. They should be led on the other side sometimes. The worst thing one sees at a show is a yearling or a two-year old being lunged on rock-hard ground for half an hour before they dare take him in the ring in a led class.

I am a great believer in long-reining young horses, although I know that some modern opinion is against it. Mr Bob Matson was one of the first to send me young horses when I started on my own. They had always been well long-reined and driven for several weeks beforehand, or longer if he thought necessary. He would always say: 'Robert, there are some four-year-olds coming on Thursday. They will be ready to be hacked and ridden away.' You could always guarantee that you could in fact back them and ride them away, as he said. But you cannot expect a sixteen-year-old-girl to long-rein a four-year-old Thoroughbred; they are far too strong and can get away from you all too easily. You need to be very careful when you drive a horse about. It is important to stand and accustom him to things. You should be able to stop and chat to someone while your horse just stands there. If he does not stand when you tell him to, then you stay there until he does so. John Moss, a great showing man, once gave me some advice about a hack I had which would not stand. 'Have your lunch on him,' said John. 'Then put your girl groom to have her lunch on him, and then the next girl groom to do the same, and just keep it up until he does stand.'

Of course, this is an old-fashioned way of doing things, but if you want results and you have got the right animal to start with, then you have got to be prepared to put in a lot of time. There are no short cuts. Too many people are looking for too many gadgets and too many short cuts. That's it in a nutshell.

CHAPTER 9

Hunter Trials, Team Cross-Country and Point-to-Pointing

Happy is he who goes out to please himself and not to h'astonish others. Mr Jorrocks.

HUNTER TRIALS

LONG BEFORE combined training became the rage hunters were regularly ridden in trials at the beginning and end of the season. There are some marvellous pre-war photographs of ladies and gentlemen in absolutely correct rat-catcher dress – bowler hats, not velvet caps, if you please – riding abreast over formidable-looking fences in hunter trials pairs contests. Some of the ladies rode these splendid trials side-saddle, and in Ireland courses included banks as well as timber and fly fences.

It is good to record that hunter trials are still flourishing in Britain, despite so many other equestrian contests now filling the fixture lists. If anything, the growth of eventing has helped; riders like competing in hunter trials to help get their horses going well across country before competing in full events.

I am inclined to be apprehensive that keen eventers will swamp hunter trials and discourage the rider with the 'ordinary hunter', but there is no sign of this so far. Most hunter trials carry a good range of restricted classes as well as the open ones. Similarly, the upsurge in the new sport of team cross-country riding, which is highly suitable to the good class hunter, has not damaged the hunter trial. Again, the hunter trial offers a splendid schooling opportunity for the young horse which is aimed at team cross-country riding later.

A splendid development is the introduction of the national hunter trials championships, sponsored by Abbey Life and involving a series of qualifying events, with a national final at Kilsby in Northamptonshire. An extremely well-built course at Kilsby offers a novice and an open alternative. There is also an 'invitation' event for leading cross-country riders, including three-day event competitors of international standard. Finally, there is a hunt event with teams of four riding together.

Kilsby is a a great gathering of hunting people from Scotland down to the West Country, and above all it is fun. The course is inviting to ride, and includes solid timber, cut and laid fences, and open water. There is a gate to be opened and shut which tests a hunter's manners and handiness in the right way, and also settles down those competitors likely to go rushing round in a tearaway manner.

I have always enjoyed hunter trials, but it must be admitted that in the past there have been some snags. Badly organised trials can cause one to wait for hours for one's turn to ride, and the scoring then tends to be erratic and unreliable. The methods of scoring have varied enormously too. Some hunts relied on a straightforward time limit, which encouraged the competition

Hunter trialling is a basic test of cross-country riding. Former international show jumper and producer of show hunters Mr David Barker, competing in the Bramham Moor trials.

The author, riding his Irish bred hunter mare Josephine in the Atherstone cross-country team event. Josephine came from the Limerick country and has been a great success in Leicestershire and Derbyshire.

to be a race against the clock; others have tried 'style judging' which involved judges at fences awarding penalties for bad style in jumping. This can cause considerable controversy, and has not always added to the sheer fun of the occasion. Badly-built courses have been another source of grouses, and in some cases have undoubtedly led to accidents. Flimsy fences are among the worst hazards, causing too many horses to take liberties and suffer bad falls as a consequence.

To overcome all these problems the British Horse Society and the Masters of Foxhounds Association have evolved rules for hunter trials which I warmly recommend to anyone seeking to run such a contest in their area, at any level. They advise that a course must be as natural as possible, and be between 2.4 and 3.2 kilometres ($1\frac{1}{2}$ to 2 miles) long, with sixteen to twenty-four obstacles. Apart from gates or stiles, the obstacles should be 'solid, fixed and imposing, and should be left as near as possible in their natural state', reinforced if necessary to remain in the same condition throughout the contest.

For novice classes the B.H.S. and M.F.H.A. recommend a maximum height of 1.06 metres (3 ft 6 ins), with 1.19 metres (3 ft 11 ins) for open classes. Spreads such as ditches or water should not exceed 2.74 metres (9 ft) in novice classes, and 3.65 metres (12 ft) in open classes. Recommended speeds are 450 to 500 metres (492 to 546 yds) per minute in the novice class, and 475 to 550 metres (519 to 600 yds) per minute in the open class.

The recommended scoring system is extremely sensible: a class should be marked in penalties, with no bonus marks and no scoring for style. In the event of two or more riders having an equal score there are several suggested methods of obtaining a result. Opening and shutting a gate should be run as a separately timed test: this could be the crucial factor in deciding the winner from two or more riders with the same overall penalties for the course. Alternatively a section of the course may be timed, including up to four obstacles, or there may be a jump-off over a shortened twisty course which may include opening and shutting a gate. The recommended rules suggest that a hunter trial course should also include a gate or stile which can

The newest cross-country sport: team cross-country riding which began at Hickstead and quickly spread throughout Britain. The Bicester Bombers team competing in Cirencester Park.

be knocked down, and they give precise advice on building such an obstacle.

There may also be alternative obstacles at some points on the course, with the most difficult alternative being free of penalties, the second most difficult receiving ten penalties, and the easiest receiving twenty. Other penalties are awarded on a precise scale for refusals, falls, errors of direction and excess time.

There is a great deal of other advice, including such essentials as the provision of ambulance and veterinary facilities. The latest rules were published in 1977, and they should do an immensely useful service in helping to raise standards and provide a much better defined system for competitors. They are a good example of the work which the B.H.S. achieves without much publicity or widespread recognition.

TEAM CROSS-COUNTRY RIDING

So far the B.H.S. has not done a great deal with the sport of team cross-country riding, although it has made a start in endeavouring to get organisers together at meetings in order to rationalise the fixture list. Ever since Mr Douglas Bunn started the first team cross-country competition in 1974 at the All-England Jumping Course at Hickstead, this sport has boomed, with imitators sprouting up all over Britain. It is an ideal sport for the rider who thoroughly enjoys the thrills of cross-country riding and wishes to use his hunter in competitions in the autumn and spring. Inevitably, some people soon began to keep horses especially for this sport, and something called a 'team cross-country horse' began to appear in advertisements in *Horse and Hound*. In fact, the vast majority of these horses are working hunters, and spend most of their time in the hunting field. The 'knockers' say that the sport is too professional now, that the prize money is too high, and that it will in the end be an unwelcome rival for point-to-point racing. I would reject all these criticisms in the main. Team cross-country riding provides an enormous amount of fun; it has improved the standards of cross-country riding and it raises a great deal of money for the hunts and for charity. The fact that a few teams have taken the trouble to raise their standards does not mean they are 'professional'. Prize-winnings may offset their costs, but the season is too short and the events too few to amount to a real bonanza for anyone. There is still a carefree jollity about the whole thing which is sadly lacking in some other equestrian areas. Team cross-country riding requires courage as well as skill, and this is excellent.

The sport attracts some splendid equestrian veterans as well as a liberal infusion of young men and women. Lord Oaksey, the former brilliant National Hunt amateur rider, and a leading journalist and TV commentator, frequently rides with his wife and others in their 'Tory Party' team (no political connotation; it is Lady Oaksey's nickname). John Oaksey says he enjoys it as much as some of his racing days, and intends to keep up his team cross-country riding for a long time yet.

The structure of team cross-country riding is varied and indeed confusing, with various championships and qualifiers up and down the country. The Zetland in Yorkshire have a splendid championship event, and so do the Meynell in Derbyshire, where they have the great advantage of one of the last

Cross-country team events usually try to reflect local conditions in the hunting field. The Condicote team splashing through water in the Worcestershire event.

Climax of the hunter 'chasing season: the Horse and Hound Hunter 'Chase Championship, held annually at the Stratford-on-Avon course. This is the first circuit in the 1977 race.

real grass hunting countries for their annual 'J.C.B.' Championship, run on old turf over superb natural fences. There is great variety in the courses and fences elsewhere, and the teams have colourful names, some barely printable. Cavalrymen, farmers, doctors, lawyers, nurses, typists – all sorts of people from many walks of life – make up the cross-country teams.

The success of cross-country team riding has re-emphasised the importance and versatility of the hunter type, and I welcome the sport because it exists in harmony with the premier sport of hunting. The Quorn Cross Country Ride at Muxlow Hill in the famous Leicestershire Monday country has one of the most delectable settings for the sport. There is a restricted class which gives the less experienced horses, and some of the heavy-weight riders, a chance to have a go, and then a splendid open class is held in the afternoon.

It has given hunting people immense pleasure to see the

Prince of Wales riding frequently in team cross-country events, with Princess Anne and Captain Mark Phillips, who have been regular competitors in these events from their inception.

Nothing could be more appropriate than the cause for which the Quorn Ride was raising money – the fighting fund to save the Vale of Belvoir from coal mining, which would mean the virtual destruction of one of the finest pieces of hunting country in the world.

Variations in courses are considerable, and so are the standards of riding them. Some improvement can be achieved here, but after its initial growth the sport is settling down to a more consistent programme of fixtures. It has a great advantage in receiving enthusiastic sponsorship for prize money and it is often highly successful as a spectator sport. Royal patronage and the participation of colourful sporting characters such as football manager and commentator Jimmy Hill have helped. Unlike racing, the team cross-country events can take place on Sunday afternoons.

Taking a drop fence the old-fashioned way, three Hunt Servants compete in the West of Yore cross-country team event: Cliff Standing (Zetland), David Anker (Sinnington) and George Cooke (Bedale and West of Yore).

Royal patronage for cross-country team events: Prince Charles rides in the Quorn event at Muxlow Hill.

The basic formula is that a team of five riders tackles a cross-country course together. There are no penalties for falls or refusals, but the deciding factor is the time of the fourth member of the team past the finishing line. Alternatively this formula can be used with teams of four, when the time of the third rider home counts. Speed is therefore important, but the formula does ensure that the contest does not simply become a race.

When the competition was started by Douglas Bunn at Hickstead teams used to attempt riding abreast at every fence and a great deal of mayhem ensured when a refuser ran down the fence, bringing down the other horses. After these early mishaps most teams rode the course more or less in single file. In 1978 Douglas Bunn therefore decided to add a new element: at certain fences only the teams had to jump absolutely abreast, and they were given penalties by the fence judges if they failed to do so. This slowed down the overall time somewhat and required rather more equitation and team riding during a round, which proved worthwhile. It also provided a better

In full flight over the Hickstead course. Competitors used to jump abreast, but soon learnt that it was better to go in single file.

spectacle for the crowds who gather at Hickstead each Easter to watch the Ride.

While team cross-country riding has the basic support of so many hunts throughout Britain I am sure the sport will continue to flourish.

POINT-TO-POINTING AND HUNTER 'CHASING

The link between the hunter and the racecourse has always been vital. Was it not from the hunting field that steeplechasing was born?

Despite dire warnings about competition from team cross-country riding, point-to-points have continued to grow. In 1978 the total number of horses entered in point-to-points rose for the first time to more than 3,000, an increase of about 600 during the previous five years. There were 184 point-to-point meetings listed that year. In addition, hunter 'chases took place at forty-two National Hunt meetings during the 1978–9 season. These races are open only to hunters qualified in the hunting field, and to amateur riders.

The regulation minimum height for a point-to-point fence is 1.29 metres (4 ft 3 ins) compared with 1.37 metres (4 ft 6 ins) on a National Hunt course. Prize money in a point-to-point is limited to £100 in an open race. In a hunter 'chase it varies from several hundreds to several thousands of pounds, for example, the Horse and Hound Hunter 'Chase Championship at the end end of the season carries prize money of some £3,000.

As we have seen earlier in Chapter 3, the H.I.S. premium stallion scheme produces a percentage of full Thoroughbred horses of which many are successful in point-to-pointing or steeplechasing under Jockey Club rules. The direct link between the hunting field and the racecourse is the system of 'qualifying'. To be eligible to race in a point-to-point or a hunter 'chase a horse must have appeared in the hunting field with one pack of hounds in the current season a minimum of eight times, and a certificate attesting to this must be obtained from the hunt concerned. Some point-to-pointers are undoubtedly hunted fairly and hard, up to Christmas, at least, when quite rightly their owners cease their regular hunting activities and keep them in training for the racing to come in the point-to-point season, from early February to the beginning of June. But a great many so-called 'hunters' in point-to-pointing are not hunted properly, at least until their racing careers are over. They make an 'appearance' in the hunting field and that is about it. Nevertheless, their owners and riders still tend to be keen hunting men and keep other horses to hunt, and the link between the two sports is still vital. The Jockey Club has warned that if hunting were abolished, point-to-points would disappear too.

The rising cost of keeping horses with professional trainers for racing under Rules has probably been a big factor in encouraging more people to 'do' their own horses at home to appear in the hunt races instead. Certainly it is not the prize money which attracts people to point-to-pointing, it is the sheer fun of the thing.

The emphasis on point-to-point racing has continued to ensure the production of full Thoroughbreds which will at some stage in their career appear in the hunting field as well as on the racecourse, and I am sure this is a beneficial factor in hunter breeding.

Hunting with the Quorn in the '78–9 season I was thrilled to realise that the horse being ridden by a young Army officer as we jogged from the meet to the first draw was none other than Ten Up, winner of a Cheltenham Gold Cup. Later that same season it was a great thrill to see that same rider, Capt James Hodges of the King's Troop R.H.A., win the Horse and Hound Grand Military Gold Cup Steeplechase with Ten Up at Sandown. Capt Hodges says the hunting field was a wonderful tonic for Ten Up after his earlier tough career on the steeple-chase course, and that he did not just make an 'appearance' with the Quorn, but was taken up to the front of the Leicestershire mounted field whenever hounds ran.

An analysis of winners of steeplechases under Rules in one

Quality hunters, all of whom could acquit themselves in the hunting field as well as on racecourse, taking part in the Horse and Hound Cup race at Stratford, in 1979.

season in Britain showed that 51% were bred in the United Kingdom, 47% in Ireland, and 2% were bred abroad. Of these totals, 58% were identified as 'purpose-bred' for 'chasing; 20% were dual purpose, that is either as a 'stayer' on the flat or a steeplechaser; and 22% were principally bred for flat racing. These figures are significant because a substantial proportion of point-to-pointers do graduate to hunter 'chasing and on to steeplechasing under Rules.

The racecourse is, of course, an excellent proving ground for horses and there is an argument that H.I.S. stallions should be selected with performance on the racecourse as a greater factor than at present, conformation currently being the most important element taken into consideration.

Not surprisingly, a beautifully turned out team at the Royal Inter-national's inter-Hunt team contest at White City. *Left to right* Miss Janet Hodgson, Mr Ronnie Marmont, and Miss Jane Walker-Okeover, representing the Meynell. Mr Marmont has a reputation as a stickler for smart turnout in hunter showing classes.

An opportunity to see a side-saddle in use over a big obstacle; usually the rider's legs are obscured by a habit. Mrs C. Alers Hanky on Cardinal Puff in the Sherston Cross Country Team event.

Some hunting folk point sorrowfully to the gulf which has widened between the half- or three-quarter-bred working hunter and the Thoroughbred point-to-pointer or hunter 'chaser. The days are virtually gone when the heavyweight man could saddle up the horse he had hunted regularly throughout the season and run it in the hunt race at the point-to-point in the spring. Point-to-pointing has become too specialised for that, although I do know a few amateur huntsmen who have actually hunted hounds on a horse which they have later raced at the end of the season.

The big factor in the change is the virtual standardisation of point-to-point fences. Instead of being natural hedges and ditches, flagged for a race, and truly representing the hunting country where the horse has 'qualified', the fences are nowadays built on a pattern similar to steeplechasing and the betting side of point-to-pointing has become significant. All this has militated against the hunter type of size and substance as well as quality, but on the whole I feel the modern trend has wrought considerable gains as well as having some drawbacks. The largest gain is that the alternative hunter, the full Thoroughbred, still has an important link with the hunting field, yet it has a job of work to do on the racecourse commensurate with the greater costs involved in breeding and keeping full Thoroughbreds. In my view, speed is a vital attribute of a top quality hunter.

If the H.I.S. eventually achieves its objective and establishes the British Hunter as a specific riding horse breed, shall we see the parting of the way between such an animal and the racecourse? I doubt it. The British are extremely good at compromises, and many a hunter will, I am sure, continue to prove equally brilliant on the racecourse and in the hunting field. The point-to-point regulations could easily be modified to accommodate the new 'breed'.

When I visited the Zetland Hunt I had a wonderful opportunity to prove that a top class Thoroughbred steeplechaser *is* often a superb hunter in the hunting field. I was mounted on Crisp, a runner-up to Red Rum in the thrilling 1974 Grand National. It will be recalled that Crisp, ridden by Richard Pitman, was in front for most of the race with a fabulous display of galloping and jumping, until he was overhauled on an agonising final run in by the great Red Rum. The time of the race, 9 minutes 1.9 seconds, broke by 19 seconds the record which Golden Miller had set 29 years earlier.

It was a daunting prospect to ride such a horse as Crisp in the hunting field, to which he was a newcomer. I heard that he objected to being clipped, and had to be anaesthetised by the vet before this could be accomplished. Further, I was warned to be a bit careful in gateways as he did not take kindly to other horses on his heels.

Mr and Mrs John Trotter, who had given Crisp a home in the Zetland country after his retirement from Fred Winter's yard, assured me that there would be no real problems as we set off to follow huntsman Cliff Standing and the Zetland

Taking a drop fence with verve and style is Mrs Michael Abrahams, wife of the Master of the West of Yore Hunt, during a cross-country team event.

Mr Reg Dennis and Sigston Queen coping with a drop fence during a
Yorkshire team event.

hounds in one of the best pieces of their fine North Yorkshire
hunting country. They were quite right. It was not long before
I forgot that I was riding a Grand National superstar. Crisp was
obviously perfectly happy in the hunting field. He galloped with
great zest, of course, but came back to me when required, and
much impressed me by the way he jumped pieces of timber off
his hocks, dealing most intelligently and carefully with in-and-
out fences. When it came to fly fences he soared and landed far
out, accelerating away much faster than the average hunter,
but clearly realising that he was not on the racecourse.

I could not fault Crisp as a hunter – proof indeed of the
adage that there is nothing a common horse can do that a
Thoroughbred cannot do better.

CHAPTER 10

People and Horses

Tell me a man's a fox-hunter and I loves 'im.
Mr Jorrocks.

IT IS merely to convey more of the atmosphere of the world of hunters and hunting that I turn finally to some of the many personalities who form a civilised and delightful band of people sharing a common interest. I cannot be comprehensive and this is by no means a catalogue of merit. There are inevitably vast omissions, since a history of all those who have contributed to the development of the hunter would be a major book in itself.

It is not only an honour, but it is also of great significance, that the Hunters' Improvement and National Light Horse Breeding Society has as its patron Her Majesty The Queen. Many people throughout the horse world have good cause to know that Her Majesty is not merely an enthusiast, but a considerable authority on Thoroughbred breeding. At Badminton Horse Trials the Queen has visited the Society's famous caravan which for so many years has flown the flag for hunter breeding at horse shows the length and breadth of England, with Major-General Sir Evelyn Fanshawe at the helm.

Queen Elizabeth The Queen Mother is a past president of the Society, and a more recent president was Princess Anne, whose achievements as a three-day event rider gave her role special meaning. Other past presidents include the Duchess of Gloucester and the Duke of Beaufort, who epitomises so much that is best in English country life. Master of his own hounds since 1924, the Duke is one of the greatest authorities on horse and hound. For forty-seven years he hunted the pack from Badminton with brilliance, and he was somewhat unusual in being an exceptional horseman as well as an outstanding hound man; the two qualities do not often go together. Known as

'Master' throughout the hunting and equestrian world, the Duke – who was born in 1900 – suffered a severe fall in the hunting field towards the end of the 1978–9 season and he was unable to attend the *Horse and Hound* Ball which he has patronised regularly throughout the postwar years. Princess Anne and Capt Mark Phillips attended the Ball which was in aid of the Hunters' Improvement Society, and we sent best wishes and condolences to the Duke who had broken a bone in his shoulder and had stitches in his head. The point of this story is that at seventy-nine years of age, Master was soon out and about again. He appeared on a horse with his hounds right at the end of the season, and presided as usual at the Badminton Three-Day Event in April when he was host to the Queen and other members of the royal family. As Sir Winston Churchill once said, 'The best thing for the inside of a man is the outside of a horse.'

There are many people rich in personality in the hunter world, and the characteristic most frequently found is a considerable resilience to the knocks and adversities of this world. Horsemen must always be prepared to remount swiftly after a fall.

Sir Evelyn Fanshawe, whom I mentioned above, was a classic example of Sir Winston Churchill's dictum. While we were wining and dining at the *Horse and Hound* Ball in aid of the H.I.S., in the same cause Sir Evelyn was making his way on a ferry to West Germany where he set up a stand at the Essen Equitana. It was just part of his regular programme of visits to propagate the Society's work.

I flew to Essen at the weekend and dined with Sir Evelyn on the Sunday night. We had a delightful evening – he was ebullient and charming as usual, full of good talk about the hunter, its past and its future. I never saw him again; two days later he died suddenly on the return trip on the ferry, aged eighty-three. 'The General' as he was known to so many in the hunter world and beyond was undoubtedly of 'the old school', but he was a true individualist and was never 'old' in any other sense. His enthusiasm, energy and sheer force of personality shone throughout his long life. He served in both world wars, and during his army career knew what it was like to hunt six days a week in the shires, and to play good polo in India. The hunting he kept up, to the end of his life. I saw him out with the Fernie in the 1977–8 season, beautifully turned out in a cutaway coat of individual and elegant style.

He took over the chairmanship of the H.I.S. Stallion Committee in 1956 and was president in 1965 and again in 1975. His annual tours of the leading horse shows and trials with the H.I.S. yellow display caravan did an incalculable service in spreading the word about the work of the Society for hunting breeding. He not only dispensed entry forms and literature, but constantly provided a fascinating and informative commentary on horse breeding. With the assistance of his secretary, Mrs Harry Townsend, he kept up the full gruelling programme of visits until the time of his death, and he had even taken delivery of a new vehicle replacing the famous caravan. Despite his age he continued to drive safely and reliably all over Britain.

Sir Evelyn was a passionate believer in the value of Thoroughbred blood in the hunter. At Essen he gestured towards a large Hanoverian horse being ridden past his stand. 'These Germans can breed pretty good show jumpers,' he said, 'but if you want horses to cross country in the hunting field or eventing there is nothing to beat our hunters with their Thoroughbred blood.'

'The General' is sadly missed, but he will never be forgotten in the hunter world.

As I write, the current president of the H.I.S. is Lt Col John Chamberlayne, a leading figure in the National Hunt scene. He has hunted all his life in his native Heythrop country, and has performed immense services for foxhunting as the Honorary Secretary of the Masters of Foxhounds Association.

The President-Elect of the H.I.S. is Lt Col Neil Foster who recently retired from the Mastership of the Grafton after twenty-seven years in office. Col Foster has a deserved reputation as one of the best men across country in the contemporary hunting field. A lightweight, he rides Thoroughbreds with extraordinary dash and an eye for country. When I remarked on his prowess he gave all the credit to his family stud groom who had kept his horses in superb condition throughout his hunting career.

Chairman of the H.I.S. is Lt Col G. A. 'Tony' Murray Smith, one of the most popular Masters in Britain, still in office in the Fernie, having previously been highly successful as Master of the Quorn.

The Council of the H.I.S. is certainly equipped with a wide range of knowledge and experience of the hunter type. Its membership includes Major Derek Allhusen, winner of Olympic gold and silver medals for eventing, and Richard Meade, winner of three Olympic gold medals in eventing. The links with racing are also strong. Capt John Macdonald-Buchanan, a long-serving Council member, became Chief Steward of the Jockey Club in 1979. His father, Major Sir Reginald Macdonald-Buchanan, is a past president of the H.I.S.

Masters of Foxhounds, past and present, are strongly represented, many of them also having experience in racing and other equestrian spheres. They include Capt Brian Fanshawe of the North Cotswold; Major Michael McEwan who used to hunt the Cattistock hounds so well in Dorset; Lt Col Sir Watkin Williams-Wynn, distinguished senior Master of the pack which bears his name in the still delectable grass country on the Welsh borders; Mr Vivian Bishop, Joint Master and huntsman of the Golden Valley since 1945; Mr Norman Crow who hunted the North Shropshire with such success; the Countess of Feversham, Joint Master of the Sinnington, one of the finest Yorkshire packs; the Hon Diana Holland-Hibbert, daughter of the renowned and much missed Lord Knutsford; Mr Archie Smith-Maxwell, for many years Joint Master of the Ledbury; and Mr W. J. B. Watson, M.R.C.V.S., former Joint Master of the Berkeley Hunt.

The Stallion Committee includes such knowledgeable figures in the breeding world as Major Andrew Hellyer and Lt Col Stephen Eve from the Cottesmore country; Mr Max Abram from North Yorkshire; and Mr Charles Cope from Gloucestershire; and there are such stalwarts as past presidents Col G. T. 'Handy' Hurrell and Mr John Cory, who was Joint Master of the Glamorgan Hunt. Mr John Sumner, the Jockey Club Steward who has played such an important role in supporting the breeding of good 'chasers, is another member of the Stallion Committee.

I have already referred to Mr Charlie Mumford who is part of the bedrock of hunter breeding at his Tea Caddy Stud in Northamptonshire. His absence from the H.I.S. Stallion Show in March, 1979, through ill health was deeply regretted by all hunter enthusiasts. It was the first time he had missed the show for many years.

Owning premium stallions is often a matter of tradition in families. The Mumfords were among those who showed at the Royal Agricultural Hall in Islington before the war. Mr Charlie Mumford began showing stallions for his father at Islington at the age of sixteen, and in those days horses travelled by train to London and were given a police escort through the streets to the Royal Agricultural Hall.

Mr Bill Manning, another highly successful premium stallion owner of the postwar years, is still spry and active, and indeed regularly contributes informative reports to *Horse and Hound* on the H.I.S. Stallion Show and the National Hunter Show at Shrewsbury.

Mr John Rawding who learnt much in his early days from Mr Manning, is nowadays successfully in hunter breeding on his own account at Manor House Farm Stud, near Tring in Hertfordshire.

The official list of judges recommended by the H.I.S. is a roll of honour from the world of the horse. The vital task of selecting the stallions at the 1979 Newmarket Show fell to Capt George Rich, who is renowned in Leicestershire as a dealer in high class horses, and Mr Thady Ryan, Master and huntsman of his family pack, the Scarteen, whose Black and Tan hounds can give you some of the most exciting times of your life across their enormous banks and ditches in Limerick and Tipperary.

The list of H.I.S. judges is indeed wide ranging. Dorian Williams, Chairman of the British Horse Society, the BBC's senior television equestrian commentator, and Joint Master of the Whaddon Chase, is one of those who gives up time in an immensely busy life to judge hunters.

It is fascinating to see the approach of specialists in allied fields, such as Mr David Nicholson, the National Hunt trainer, judging hunters in the main ring of the Royal at Stoneleigh.

Such authorities as Col Foster, Mr Chubb Castle or Mr John

Daniell are well known in the centre of the big rings, judging major championships. One barrier was broken in 1976 when Mrs George Gibson became the first woman invited to judge at the Stallion Show at Newmarket. The same year Mrs Gibson became Joint Master of the Cottesmore where she has hunted all her life. Her husband heads a well-known veterinary practice at Oakham, their son Michael is another partner in the practice, and their elder son David runs the Barleythorpe Stud. Mrs Gibson is a good example of the immense practical experience which is still, thank heaven, the main asset of leading people in the hunter world.

Another lady judge who exemplifies all-round experience of breeding, producing and riding hunters is Mrs Hugh Gingell, who has an extraordinary record as Master and huntsman of the Cambridgeshire Harriers since 1942. Apart from being one of the nicest people in the equestrian world, Mrs Gingell has a remarkable air of never changing unflappability, and she has a great eye for judging young stock. Her own beautifully produced show hunters have won shoals of major prizes.

Among the professional producers of show hunters, only one woman has emerged regularly to beat the men – Miss Ruth McMullen. From her yard in Norfolk Miss McMullen has produced horses for owners including Paul Rackham, Master of the Suffolk Hunt, and Lady Zinnia Pollock, who is due to succeed as Joint Master of the Whaddon Chase with Mr David Barker in the 1980–81 season.

David Barker made the unusual transition from top international show-jumping rider to a producer and rider of show horses. These included Lady Zinnia Pollock's Swanbourne which won the Championship at the Royal International Horse Show in 1978. David farms in the Whaddon Chase country and is to hunt these hounds himself when Albert Buckle relinquishes the horn after twenty-six years at the end of the 1979–80 season.

A great loss among professional show-men was Jack Gittins, who died in the saddle at the Royal Dublin Show in 1977 after a lifetime with horses, including many years at the top of the show hunter world. He rode six supreme champions at Dublin, appearing for Nat Galway-Greer, who found so many great horses which went on to achieve still more successes in England after first shining at Ballsbridge. Jack was a wonderful personality, and is much missed by all.

I have already referred at length to Robert Oliver, and contemporary with him is David Tatlow whose yard at Stow-in-the-Wold in the centre of the Heythrop country is the nursery for so many good hunters. David was born to succeed in the horse world, being the son of a great show-man, Mr Harry Tatlow.

Having had a most successful early career in point-to-pointing and 'chasing, David is a great chap for producing horses which can really perform over fences. In the winter months nowadays he and his attractive wife Barbara enliven their hunting season still more by riding in team cross-country rides. The Prince of Wales has regularly taken part in their winning team, the Ratcatchers.

The Midlands is traditionally the area for some of the great producers of hunters. For cheerfulness and hard work it is difficult to beat Mr L. S. 'Tub' Ivens from the Grafton country, who has been immensely successful with in-hand and ridden stock. His Sammy Dasher won the Prince of Wales Cup at Shrewsbury in 1974, and 'Tub' has often ridden champions in the saddle classes as well. Like all the show-men, he adores his hunting in the winter months, and I have had great fun in the Grafton country mounted on some 'good sorts' from Tub's yard.

It is not surprising that the Grafton has such a tradition of producing good horses and good men. Before and just after the war it still had a reputation as being one of the biggest countries to cross in the British Isles. The huge Northamptonshire hedges guard formidable ditches, and it rides deeper than Leicestershire. Unfortunately the change to arable farming from pasture has gobbled up much of the country under the plough nowadays, the fate of so many other former grass hunting countries. But the traditions of good horses from the Grafton lives on, as you will see in point-to-point results as well as the show hunter ring.

Vincent Toulson, mentioned earlier in connection with Prince's Street, has a fine business, making and producing quality horses near Melton Mowbray. He was a highly successful amateur rider in point-to-points and under Rules, but imbibed the showing lore from his father Mr Charles Toulson who showed before the war at Olympia. Like so many successful people in the horse world, Vin Toulson is fortunate in having the practical help of a marvellous wife who also shows hunters with considerable success in the major classes.

Down in the south, the name Trigg is of special significance in hunter showing. Roy Trigg, son of Robert Trigg from Fareham in Hampshire, is a highly successful show-man. He started out by working for Dick Hunt in the Portman country's wonderful grass vale, west of Blandford, and adjoining the Blackmore Vale. Horses have to perform genuinely in this country to get across the big hedges. Later Roy worked for the late Mr Gerry Langford, the veterinary surgeon at Lingfield who had such a great reputation in Surrey. I recall Gerry, late in life, riding young horses with the Mid-Surrey Drag Hunt with a wonderfully relaxed but effective style. We had a splendid line from Staffhurst Wood which went south and finished on Gerry's land near Lingfield where there was a mouth-watering stretch of grass and superb fly fences. It was difficult to 'strike them right' when foxhunting, but the Drag could ensure that you did not miss one, and Gerry was among those who showed us the way.

Roy Trigg later set up a farm and yard in Sussex where he has remained, and is still a regular figure in the major show rings.

Donald Owen from Kent is another successful producer of show horses in the postwar years; he now farms in Buckinghamshire, in the Whaddon Chase country. He is one of those who did not have a particularly horsy background, but made his own way after learning to ride at a local riding school. He has a knack of taking immense pains with individual horses and has been highly successful with hacks, winning the Hack of the Year award at Wembley with, amazingly, a four-year-old, Feudal Knight.

For sheer style as well as expertise Count Robert Orssich could not be beaten in hunter showing and in the production of hacks and other show animals. Son of an Austrian cavalry officer, and with a remarkable inheritance of the standards of equitation which were so high in Imperial Austria, Count Orssich contributed much to the British showing scene. A co-founder of the Royal Windsor Horse Show with its chairman, Mr Geoffrey Cross, the Count lives in retirement near Windsor, but continues to contribute much through his advice and guidance to many. He has recently contributed a number of immensely interesting articles to *Horse and Hound*.

It can be seen, in the story of the hunter, that one golden thread of common interest runs through the widely varying activities that this remarkable type of horse can perform for man. Its name is derived from the principal sport for which our forefathers bred and produced this wonderful animal. Most of the people mentioned in this book would agree with the great hunting poet, G. J. Whyte-Melville, that the best of their fun they owed to horse and hound.

This memorable phrase comes from his poem 'The Good Grey Mare', which is an old man's expression of delight in the fun he has had in the hunting field on his favourite horse.

The last verse of the poem sums up the link between man and the hunter – and its true environment, the hunting field:

> I have lived my life – I am nearly done –
> I have play'd the game all round;
> But I freely admit that the best of my fun
> I owe it to horse and hound.
> With a hopeful heart and a conscience clear,
> I can laugh in your face, Black Care;
> Though you're hovering near, there's no room for you here,
> On the back of my good grey mare.

Useful Addresses, Breed Societies, Etc.

Arab Horse Society: Lt Col J. Denney, Sackville Lodge, Lye Green, Crowborough, Sussex. Tel. Crowborough 5448

British Horse Society: British Equestrian Centre, Kenilworth, Warwickshire, CV8 2LR. Tel. Coventry 27192

British Irish Draught Horse Society: Mrs D. Holmes, The Cuttings, Reepham Road, Bawdeswell, Norfolk.

Cleveland Bay Horse Society: J. F. Stephenson, York Livestock Centre, Murton, York, YO1 3UF. Tel. York 489 731

Connemara Pony Breeders' Society: J. Killeen, 9 Ardna Mara, Salthill, Galway, Eire.

English Connemara Pony Society: Mrs Barthrop, The Quinta, Bentley, Farnham, Surrey. Tel. Bentley 3159

Hunters' Improvement and National Light Horse Society: G. W. Evans, National Westminster Bank Chambers, 8 Market Square, Westerham, Kent. Tel. Westerham 63867

Irish Horse Board (Bord na gCapall): Blessington Road, Tallaght, Co. Dublin, Ireland. Tel. (01) 510122

Ladies Side-saddle Association: Mrs V. Francis, 28 Featherbed Lane, Addington, Croydon, Surrey. Tel. 01–788 3642

Thoroughbred Breeders' Association: S. G. Sheppard, 168 High Street, Newmarket, Suffolk. Tel. Newmarket 61321

Welsh Pony and Cob Society: T. E. Roberts, 32 North Parade, Aberystwyth, Cards. Tel. Aberystwyth 617501

ACKNOWLEDGEMENTS

Photographs were kindly supplied as follows: Castle Studio, Nether Stowey 74; Charles Donaldson, Dover 73; Charles C. Fennell, Dublin 108; Frank Fennell, Dublin 106, 108; David A. Guiver, Wallington, Surrey 129; Julian Hasler, Tetbury 159; Clive Hiles, Wembley 75; Kit Houghton, Bridgwater, Somerset 15, 59, 112, 116, 148–9; John F. Hughes, Rugby 20–21, 24–25, International News Photos 69; Leslie Lane, Burgess Hill 36–37, 45, 46, 52, 56, 61, 64, 70, 71, 105, 110, 124, 130, 155; Bob Langrish, Stroud, Glos. 134, 136, 137, 138, 140, 141, 142, 143; Les Mayall, Haye-on-Wye 78; Frank H. Meads, Brackley 13, 28, 43, 47, 55, 81, 82, 83, 88, 90–91, 95, 101, 121, 152, 154; Jim Meads, Brackley 14, 55, 147, 157; 'Monty', Birmingham 51, 68, 104, 122, 126, 146; H. S. Newsham, Stourport 151; Roy Parker, Scarborough 153, 161, 162; Press Association, London 118–19; Sport & General Press Agency, London 113, 128, 158; Fiona Vigors, Upper Lambourn 48.